ADVANCED PLACEMENT
ECONOMICS
MACROECONOMICS

Student Resource Manual

4th Edition
Margaret A. Ray

COUNCIL FOR
**Economic
Education**

Teaching Opportunity

Author

Margaret A. Ray is a professor of economics and director of the Center for Economic Education at the University of Mary Washington. She taught Advanced Placement Economics at Collegiate School in Richmond, Virginia, in 2002–2003 and was an economist and director of economic education at the Federal Reserve Bank of Richmond. Margaret has been a reader, table leader, and question leader for the AP Economic Examinations from 1993 to the present and and she received the Excellence in Teaching Economics award from the Council for Economic Education for her work developing curriculum for teaching introductory economics.

Contributing Author

Gary L. Stone, author of *Advanced Placement Economics Microeconomics* and contributor to Unit 1, is a professor of economics and director of the Center for Economic Education at Winthrop University. He has conducted numerous workshops for AP Economics teachers and has been a reader and table leader for the AP Economics Examinations for over two decades. Gary received the Bessie B. Moore Service Award from the National Association of Economic Educators for his work in economic education with K–12 teachers in the United States and other countries.

Content Consultant

Dennis Placone is professor emeritus of economics and director of the Center for Economic Education at Clemson University. He has more than 35 years of teaching, research, and administrative experience at Clemson, and has conducted workshops for K–12 teachers including AP teachers since 1989. He served as chair of the AP Economics Test Development Committee from 1997–2003.

Project Director

Kevin Gotchet is the director for the Excellence in Economic Education program. He has been with the Council for Economic Education for more than eight years and has taken a leading role in several CEE initiatives.

Funding

The Council for Economic Education gratefully acknowledges the funding of this publication by the U.S. Department of Education, Office of Innovation and Improvement, Excellence in Economic Education: Advancing K–12 Economic & Financial Education Nationwide grant award U215B100002. The contents of this book developed under the grant from the Department of Education do not necessarily represent the policy of the Department of Education, and you should not assume endorsement by the federal government.

ISBN: 978-156183-668-0

Contents

Contents

MACROECONOMICS

Basic Economic Concepts

Unit 1

■ Scarcity exists because we have limited resources and unlimited wants. No society has ever had enough resources to produce all the goods and services its members wanted.

■ Goods and services are produced from resources. These resources—land, labor, capital, and entrepreneurship—are limited.

■ Scarcity requires people to make choices. If we use scarce resources for one purpose, we cannot use them for another.

■ Opportunity cost is the forgone benefit of the next best alternative when resources are used for one purpose rather than another.

■ Because of scarcity, every decision has an opportunity cost.

■ Economic costs take account of the opportunity cost of doing one thing rather than another.

■ Economic costs include explicit costs and implicit costs. Explicit costs are expenditures for something. Implicit costs are the opportunity costs of using your own resources rather than selling them to someone else. Both implicit and explicit costs are opportunity costs.

■ Using free goods does not involve opportunity cost because free goods are available in unlimited quantities.

■ Economics is concerned with marginal decision making. In economics, "making decisions at the margin" is very important. Marginal choices involve the effects of additions and subtractions from the current situation. We compare the marginal benefit of an extra unit of an activity with that unit's marginal cost.

■ A production possibilities curve can be used to illustrate scarcity, choice, and opportunity cost graphically.

■ The slope of a production possibilities curve shows the opportunity cost of producing another unit of one good in terms of the amount of the other good that must be given up.

■ Because resources are scarce, using them efficiently allows us to get the most from them. Efficiency is increased through specialization and trade. Economists use the concept of comparative advantage to explain why trade takes place between countries and between individuals. This concept is based on the differences in producers' opportunity costs of producing goods and services.

■ The law of comparative advantage shows how everyone can gain through trade.

■ Economic theory is useful in analyzing and understanding the world around us.

■ The test of an economic theory is its ability to predict correctly the future consequences of economic actions.

■ The broad social goals of a society influence decisions about how best to use resources.

■ Markets bring together buyers and sellers of a good or service.

■ The law of demand states that buyers will want more of an item at a low price than at a high price, other things being equal.

■ The law of supply states that sellers will provide more of an item at a high price than at a low price, other things being equal.

■ The equilibrium price is the price at which the quantity demanded of an item equals the quantity supplied. That quantity is called the equilibrium quantity.

■ Shifts in the market demand and supply curves result in new values of the equilibrium price and quantity. Understanding what causes shifts in the demand and supply curves is an important part of knowing how a market operates.

■ There are three important goals for the macroeconomy: full employment, price stability, and economic growth.

■ A business cycle describes the ups and downs of economic activity over a period of years.

■ The phases of the business cycle are expansion (recovery), peak, contraction (recession), and trough.

Do You Think Like an Economist?

Circle T for *true* or F for *false* in the statements that follow.

T F 1. Because it is desirable, sunshine is scarce.

T F 2. Because it is limited, polio is scarce.

T F 3. Because water covers three-fourths of the earth's surface and is renewable, it cannot be considered scarce.

T F 4. The main cost of going to college is tuition, room, and board.

T F 5. If mass transportation fares are raised, almost everyone will take the trains anyway.

T F 6. You get what you pay for.

T F 7. If someone makes an economic gain, someone else loses.

T F 8. If one nation produces everything better than another nation, there is no economic reason for these two nations to trade.

T F 9. A nonregulated monopoly tends to charge the highest possible price.

T F 10. A business owner's decision to show more care for consumers is a decision to accept lower levels of profits.

Scarcity, Opportunity Cost, and Production Possibilities Curves

The primary economic problem facing all individuals, families, businesses, and nations is the scarcity of resources: There simply are not enough resources to satisfy the unlimited wants for goods and services. Scarcity necessitates choice. Consuming or producing more of one thing means consuming or producing less of something else. The opportunity cost of using scarce resources for one thing instead of something else is often represented in graphical form as a *production possibilities curve* (PPC). A nation's PPC shows how many units of two goods or services the nation can produce in one year if it uses its resources fully and efficiently. This activity uses the PPC to illustrate how scarcity requires choices and the opportunity cost of those choices.

Part A: Basic Production Possibilities Curves

Figure 1-2.1 shows a basic PPC for the production of Goods A and B. Use Figure 1-2.1 to answer the questions that follow.

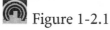 Figure 1-2.1
A Linear Production Possibilities Curve

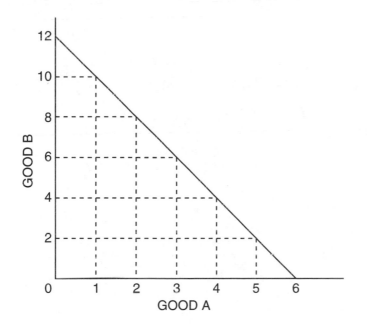

1. Assume the economy represented by Figure 1-2.1 is presently producing 12 units of Good B and 0 units of Good A:

   (A) The opportunity cost of increasing production of Good A from 0 units to 1 unit is the loss of _____ unit(s) of Good B.

   (B) The opportunity cost of increasing production of Good A from 1 unit to 2 units is the loss of _____ unit(s) of Good B.

   (C) The opportunity cost of increasing production of Good A from 2 units to 3 units is the loss of _____ unit(s) of Good B.

   (D) This is an example of (*constant / increasing / decreasing / zero*) opportunity cost per unit for Good A.

Figure 1-2.2 contains a typical PPC often used by economists. This PPC is concave to the origin; it gets steeper as the country moves out along its horizontal axis. Use Figure 1-2.2 to answer the questions that follow.

Figure 1-2.2
A Concave Production Possibilities Curve

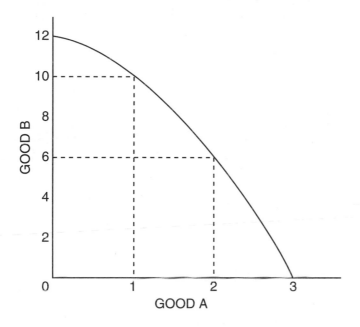

2. If the economy represented in Figure 1-2.2 is presently producing 12 units of Good B and 0 units of Good A:

(A) The opportunity cost of increasing production of Good A from 0 units to 1 unit is the loss of _____ unit(s) of Good B.

(B) The opportunity cost of increasing production of Good A from 1 unit to 2 units is the loss of _____ unit(s) of Good B.

(C) The opportunity cost of increasing production of Good A from 2 units to 3 units is the loss of _____ unit(s) of Good B.

(D) This is an example of (*constant / increasing / decreasing / zero*) opportunity cost per unit for Good A.

Part B: Understanding the Shape of a Concave PPC

The "law of increasing opportunity cost" explains why the typical PPC is concave to the origin (bowed outward). Figure 1-2.3 shows the PPC for the country of Costica. The country currently operates at point A and produces 75 million units of civilian goods and 2 million units of military goods. If the country decides to increase its military provision to 3 million units, it must give up only 5 million units in civilian goods because certain factories are easily converted from civilian production to military production. However, if Costica decides it must continue to increase its military production, the opportunity cost of doing so increases because now it is more difficult to convert other factories to military production. Resources are not equally well suited to the production of all goods. The opportunity cost of increasing military output from 6 million units to 7 million units (point C to point D) has increased to 15 million units in civilian goods. This increasing opportunity cost is reflected in the steeper slope of the PPC as the country produces more military goods and fewer civilian goods.

Figure 1-2.3
Showing the Law of Increasing Opportunity Cost

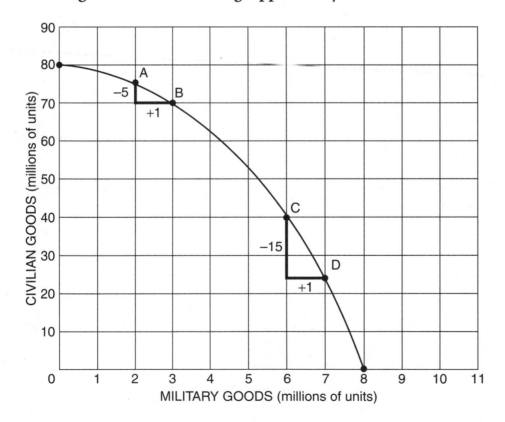

Advanced Placement Economics Macroeconomics: Student Resource Manual © Council for Economic Education, New York, N.Y.

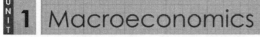
Part C: Drawing Various PPCs

Use the following axes to draw the type of curve that illustrates the label above each graph.

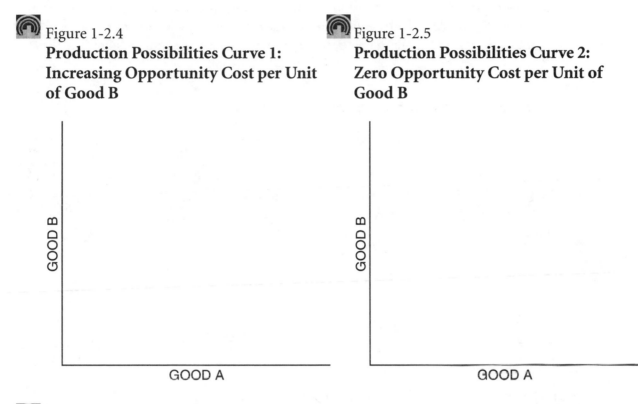

Figure 1-2.4

Production Possibilities Curve 1: Increasing Opportunity Cost per Unit of Good B

GOOD B

GOOD A

Figure 1-2.5

Production Possibilities Curve 2: Zero Opportunity Cost per Unit of Good B

GOOD B

GOOD A

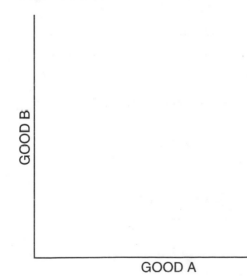

Figure 1-2.6

Production Possibilities Curve 3: Constant Opportunity Cost per Unit of Good B

GOOD B

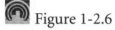

GOOD A

Part D: Economic Growth

Over time, most countries see an increase in their ability to produce goods and services. This "economic growth" is shown as an outward shift of the PPC and results from a variety of factors, including improved technology, better education, and the discovery of new resources. Use Figure 1-2.7 to answer the next five questions. Each question starts with Curve BE as a country's PPC.

Figure 1-2.7
Production Possibilities Curve: Capital Goods and Consumer Goods

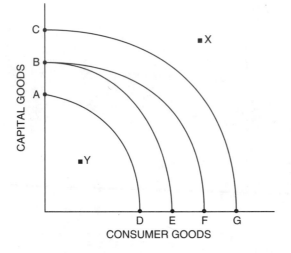

3. Suppose there is a major technological breakthrough in the consumer-goods industry, and the new technology is widely adopted. Which curve in the diagram would represent the new PPC? (Indicate the curve you choose with two letters.) _____

4. Suppose a new government comes into power and forbids the use of automated machinery and modern production techniques in all industries. Which curve in the diagram would represent the new PPC? (Indicate the curve you choose with two letters.) _____

5. Suppose massive new sources of oil and coal are found within the economy, and there are major technological innovations in both industries. Which curve in the diagram would represent the new PPC? (Indicate the curve you choose with two letters.) _____

6. If BE represents a country's current PPC, what can you say about a point like X? (Write a brief statement.)

7. If BE represents a country's current PPC, what can you say about a point like Y? (Write a brief statement.)

Use Figure 1-2.8 to answer the next three questions.

Figure 1-2.8
Production Possibilities Curve: Economic Growth

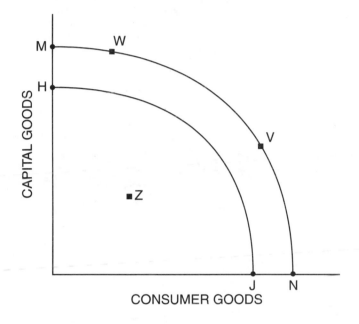

8. What change could cause the PPC to shift from the original curve (HJ) to the new curve (MN)?

9. Under what conditions might an economy be operating at Point Z?

10. Why might a government implement a policy to move the economy from Point V to Point W?

Determining Comparative Advantage

Voluntary trade between two individuals or two countries occurs if both parties feel that they will benefit. Producers have an incentive to make products for which they have a lower opportunity cost than other producers. When both producers specialize according to their *comparative advantage*, they increase the total amount of goods and services that are available for consumption. To determine who has a comparative advantage in producing a particular item, we need to calculate each producer's opportunity costs of creating the items. The way we calculate opportunity cost depends on how the productivity data are expressed.

There are two ways to measure productivity: the "input method" and the "output method." We can calculate the quantity of output produced from a given amount of inputs, or we can measure the amount of inputs necessary to create one unit of output. Examples of output are tons of wheat per acre, miles per gallon, words per minute, apples per tree, and televisions produced per hour. Examples of input are number of hours to do a job, number of gallons of paint to paint a house, and number of acres to feed a horse. We will work through an example that expresses productivity from the perspectives of an input measure and an output measure.

Part A: Two Approaches to Comparative Advantage

Student Alert: In using these models to determine the lower opportunity costs from both an input and output viewpoint, you must pay attention to the format of the chart. It makes a difference!

Input Method

The "input method" provides data on the amount of resources needed to produce one unit of output. Table 1-3.1 gives productivity information for Ted and Nancy.

 Table 1-3.1
Productivity Data Using the Input Method

	Time required to produce one radio	Time required to produce one bushel of wheat
Ted	20 minutes	5 minutes
Nancy	30 minutes	15 minutes

Ted has an *absolute advantage* in the production of both radios and wheat because he uses fewer resources (time) to produce each item than does Nancy. Even though this might suggest that Ted cannot benefit from trade with Nancy, our examination of the opportunity costs of production will show that is not the case.

Table 1-3.2 shows the opportunity costs for each producer. To find the opportunity cost of producing one radio, the amount of resources it takes to produce a radio goes *above* the amount of resources that it takes to produce a bushel of wheat.

Table 1-3.2
Opportunity Cost of Producing Radios and Wheat

	Opportunity cost of producing one radio	Opportunity cost of producing one bushel of wheat
Ted	$1 \text{ radio} = \dfrac{20 \text{ minutes}}{5 \text{ minutes}} = 4 \text{ bushels}$	$1 \text{ wheat} = \dfrac{5 \text{ minutes}}{20 \text{ minutes}} = \text{¼ radio}$
Nancy	$1 \text{ radio} = \dfrac{30 \text{ minutes}}{15 \text{ minutes}} = 2 \text{ bushels}$	$1 \text{ wheat} = \dfrac{15 \text{ minutes}}{30 \text{ minutes}} = \text{½ radio}$

In the 20 minutes it takes Ted to produce one radio, he instead could have produced four bushels of wheat. Instead of producing one radio in 30 minutes, Nancy could have produced two bushels of wheat. The fact that Nancy has the lower opportunity cost of producing radios means she has the comparative advantage in radios.

In the five minutes he needs to produce one bushel of wheat, Ted could have made ¼ of a radio. Nancy's opportunity cost of producing one bushel of wheat is ½ of a radio. Because his sacrifice in producing a radio is less than Nancy's, Ted has the comparative advantage in wheat production.

If Ted specializes in wheat production while Nancy specializes in radio production, their combined output of radios and wheat will be larger than it would be if each person produced both products.

Output Method

The "output method" gives data on the amount of output that can be produced with a given amount of an input. Now let's take this same set of productivity data and turn it into an output format. To do this, we ask how many units of an item the producers can create with a given amount of resources. Let's suppose that both producers have one hour to produce each product. Table 1-3.3 shows how many radios and how many bushels of wheat each producer can make in one hour. From this output viewpoint, you once again see that Ted has the absolute advantage in the production of both products. With the same amount of resources (one hour of labor), he can produce more radios and more wheat than Nancy.

Table 1-3.3
Productivity Data Using the Output Method

	Radios produced per hour	Wheat produced per hour
Ted	$\dfrac{60 \text{ minutes}}{20 \text{ minutes}} = 3 \text{ radios}$	$\dfrac{60 \text{ minutes}}{5 \text{ minutes}} = 12 \text{ bushels}$
Nancy	$\dfrac{60 \text{ minutes}}{30 \text{ minutes}} = 2 \text{ radios}$	$\dfrac{60 \text{ minutes}}{15 \text{ minutes}} = 4 \text{ bushels}$

But what about the opportunity cost to produce each item? Check out Table 1-3.4, which shows how to calculate each producer's opportunity cost of the two items. To find Ted's opportunity cost of producing one radio, the number of radios he can produce in one hour goes *under* the number of bushels of wheat he can produce in that same time frame.

Table 1-3.4
Opportunity Cost of Producing Radios and Wheat

	Opportunity cost of producing one radio	Opportunity cost of producing one bushel of wheat
Ted	3 radios = 1 hour = 12 bushels 1 radio = 12/3 = 4 bushels	12 bushels = 1 hour = 3 radios 1 bushel = 3/12 = ¼ radio
Nancy	2 radios = 1 hour = 4 bushels 1 radio = 4/2 = 2 bushels	4 bushels = 1 hour = 2 radios 1 bushel = 2/4 = ½ radio

Because Ted's cost per radio is four bushels of wheat, whereas Nancy's cost is only two bushels, we know Nancy has the comparative advantage in producing radios. Ted has the comparative advantage in wheat production since he has the lower opportunity cost of producing a bushel of wheat (¼ radio compared to Nancy's ½ radio). Does this sound familiar? This is the same result we reached using the input method.

The differences in opportunity costs define the limits of a trade in which both parties will benefit. If Nancy specializes in radio production, she will accept no less than two bushels of wheat for one radio. Ted will pay no more than four bushels of wheat per radio. Thus, the "terms of trade" acceptable to both producers must lie in the range between two bushels for one radio and four bushels for one radio. For example, suppose they agree to trade one radio for three bushels of wheat. By producing and trading one radio to Ted, Nancy will have a net gain of one bushel. Her opportunity cost of producing the radio is two bushels and she receives three bushels in return for the radio. Because his opportunity cost of producing one bushel is ¼ radio, Ted's opportunity cost of producing the three bushels, which he trades to Nancy, is ¾ radio. Thus, the trade gives Ted a net gain of ¼ radio. Both producers gain by specializing according to their comparative advantage.

When it comes to producing wheat, Ted would have to receive at least ¼ of a radio in trade for a bushel of wheat. Nancy would require at least ½ of a radio before she would trade a bushel of wheat. The acceptable terms of trade would be found between ¼ radio and ½ radio per bushel of wheat.

The output data in Table 1-3.3 can be used to create production possibility frontiers for Ted and Nancy to show the combinations of radios and wheat each can produce in one hour of work. See Figure 1-3.1.

Figure 1-3.1
Production Possibilities Curves for Ted and Nancy

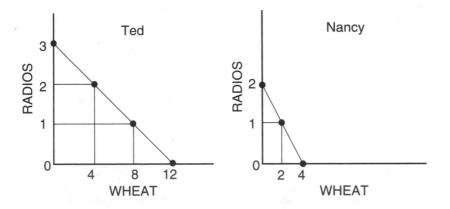

Part B: Comparative Advantage Exercises

For each of the following scenarios, answer the questions following the chart. The first problem is answered for you.

1. Anna and Barry can grow the following amounts of potatoes and cabbage with a week of labor.

	Potatoes per week	Cabbage per week
Anna	100 units	200 units
Barry	120 units	150 units

(A) Is this an example of an *input* problem or an *output* problem?

(B) What is the opportunity cost for each producer in making these products?

(1) Anna's opportunity cost of producing a unit of potatoes is _____ units of cabbage.

(2) Barry's opportunity cost of producing a unit of potatoes is _____ units of cabbage.

(3) Anna's opportunity cost of producing a unit of cabbage is _____ units of potatoes.

(4) Barry's opportunity cost of producing a unit of cabbage is _____ units of potatoes.

(C) Who has the comparative advantage in producing potatoes? _____

(D) Who has the comparative advantage in producing cabbage? _____

Note: In this example, each producer has the absolute advantage in producing one item: Barry in potatoes and Anna in cabbage. That might not be the case in the other examples.

2. Henry and John are fishermen who catch bass and catfish. This chart shows how many of each type of fish they can catch in one day.

	Bass	Catfish
Henry	4 bass	6 catfish
John	24 bass	12 catfish

(A) Is this an example of an *input* problem or an *output* problem?

(B) What is the opportunity cost for each person in catching these fish?

(1) Henry's opportunity cost of catching 1 bass is _____ catfish.

(2) John's opportunity cost of catching 1 bass is _____ catfish.

(3) Henry's opportunity cost of catching 1 catfish is _____ bass.

(4) John's opportunity cost of catching 1 catfish is _____ bass.

(C) Who has the comparative advantage in catching bass? _____

(D) Who has the comparative advantage in catching catfish? _____

3. This chart shows how many days it takes the ABC Corporation and the XYZ Corporation to produce one unit of cars and one unit of planes.

	Cars	Planes
ABC Corp.	8 days	10 days
XYZ Corp.	15 days	12 days

(A) Is this an example of an *input* problem or an *output* problem?

(B) What is the opportunity cost for each corporation in producing these goods?

    (1) ABC's opportunity cost of producing a unit of cars is _____ units of planes.

    (2) XYZ's opportunity cost of producing a unit of cars is _____ units of planes.

    (3) ABC's opportunity cost of producing a units of planes is _____ units of cars.

    (4) XYZ's opportunity cost of producing a unit of planes is _____ units of cars.

(C) Who has the comparative advantage in producing cars? _____

(D) Who has the comparative advantage in producing planes? _____

4. Here are the numbers of acres needed in India and China to produce 100 bushels of corn or 100 bushels of rice each month.

	India	China
Corn	9 acres	8 acres
Rice	3 acres	2 acres

(A) Is this an example of an *input* problem or an *output* problem?

(B) What is the opportunity cost for each country in producing these goods?

    (1) India's opportunity cost of growing 100 bushels of corn is _____ bushels of rice.

    (2) China's opportunity cost of growing 100 bushels of corn is _____ bushels of rice.

    (3) India's opportunity cost of growing 100 bushels of rice is _____ bushels of corn.

    (4) China's opportunity cost of growing 100 bushels of rice is _____ bushels of corn.

(C) Who has the comparative advantage in growing corn? _____

(D) Who has the comparative advantage in growing rice? _____

5. This chart shows how many cans of olives and bottles of olive oil can be produced in Zaire and Colombia from one ton of olives.

	Zaire	Colombia
Olives	60 cans	24 cans
Olive oil	10 bottles	8 bottles

(A) Is this an example of an *input* problem or an *output* problem?

(B) What is the opportunity cost for each country in producing these goods?

    (1) Zaire's opportunity cost of producing 1 can of olives is _____ bottles of olive oil.

    (2) Colombia's opportunity cost of producing 1 can of olives is _____ bottles of olive oil.

    (3) Zaire's opportunity cost of producing 1 bottle of olive oil is _____ cans of olives.

    (4) Colombia's opportunity cost of producing 1 bottle of olive oil is _____ cans of olives.

(C) Who has the comparative advantage in producing olives? _____

(D) Who has the comparative advantage in producing olive oil? _____

6. Here are the numbers of hours needed in Redland and Blueland to produce a unit of televisions and a unit of computers.

	Televisions	Computers
Redland	18 hours	6 hours
Blueland	16 hours	4 hours

(A) Is this an example of an *input* problem or an *output* problem?

(B) What is the opportunity cost for each country in producing these goods?

(1) Redland's opportunity cost of producing 1 unit of televisions is _____ units of computers.

(2) Blueland's opportunity cost of producing 1 unit of televisions is _____ units of computers.

(3) Redland's opportunity cost of producing 1 unit of computers is _____ units of televisions.

(4) Blueland's opportunity cost of producing 1 unit of computers is _____ units of televisions.

(C) Who has the comparative advantage in producing televisions? _____

(D) Who has the comparative advantage in producing computers? _____

Demand Curves, Movements along Demand Curves, and Shifts in Demand Curves

Part A: A Change in Demand versus a Change in Quantity Demanded

! *Student Alert:* **The distinction between a "change in demand" and a "change in quantity demanded" is very important!**

Table 1-4.1 shows the market demand for a hypothetical product: Greebes. Study the data and plot the demand for Greebes on the graph in Figure 1-4.1. Label the demand curve D, and answer the questions that follow.

Table 1-4.1
Demand for Greebes

Price (per Greebe)	Quantity demanded per week (millions of Greebes)
$0.10	350
$0.15	300
$0.20	250
$0.25	200
$0.30	150
$0.35	100
$0.40	50
$0.45	0

Figure 1-4.1
Demand for Greebes

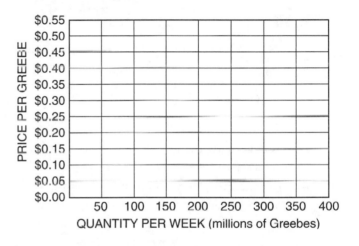

1. The data for demand curve D indicate that at a price of $0.30 per Greebe, buyers would be willing to buy _____ million Greebes. All other things held constant, if the price of Greebes increased to $0.40 per Greebe, buyers would be willing to buy _____ million Greebes. Such a change would be a decrease in (*demand / quantity demanded*). All other things held constant, if the price of Greebes decreased to $0.20, buyers would be willing to buy _____ million Greebes. Such a change would be called an increase in (*demand / quantity demanded*).

Now, let's suppose there is a change in federal income-tax rates that affects the disposable income of Greebe buyers. This change in the *ceteris paribus* (all else being equal) conditions underlying the original demand for Greebes will result in a new set of data, shown in Table 1-4.2. Study these new data, and add the new demand curve for Greebes to the graph in Figure 1-4.1. Label the new demand curve D_1 and answer the questions that follow.

Table 1-4.2

New Demand for Greebes

Price (per Greebe)	Quantity demanded per week (millions of Greebes)
$0.05	300
$0.10	250
$0.15	200
$0.20	150
$0.25	100
$0.30	50

2. Comparing the new demand curve (D_1) with the original demand curve (D), we can say that the change in the demand for Greebes results in a shift of the demand curve to the (*left / right*). Such a shift indicates that at each of the possible prices shown, buyers are now willing to buy a (*smaller / larger*) quantity; and at each of the possible quantities shown, buyers are willing to offer a (*higher / lower*) maximum price. The cause of this demand curve shift was a(n) (*increase / decrease*) in tax rates that (*increased / decreased*) the disposable income of Greebe buyers.

Now, let's suppose that there is a dramatic change in people's tastes and preferences for Greebes. This change in the *ceteris paribus* conditions underlying the original demand for Greebes will result in a new set of data, shown in Table 1-4.3. Study these new data, and add the new demand curve for Greebes to the graph in Figure 1-4.1. Label the new demand curve D_2 and answer the questions that follow.

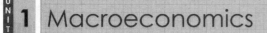 Table 1-4.3
New Demand for Greebes

Price (per Greebe)	Quantity demanded per week (millions of Greebes)
$0.20	350
$0.25	300
$0.30	250
$0.35	200
$0.40	150
$0.45	100
$0.50	50

3. Comparing the new demand curve (D_2) with the original demand curve (D), we can say that the change in the demand for Greebes results in a shift of the demand curve to the (*left / right*). Such a shift indicates that at each of the possible prices shown, buyers are now willing to buy a (*smaller / larger*) quantity; and at each of the possible quantities shown, buyers are willing to offer a (*lower / higher*) maximum price. The cause of this shift in the demand curve was a(n) (*increase / decrease*) in people's tastes and preferences for Greebes.

Part B: Do You Get It?

Now, to test your understanding, choose the answer you think is the best in each of the following multiple-choice questions.

4. All other things held constant, which of the following would *not* cause a change in the demand (shift in the demand curve) for motorcycles?

    (A) A decrease in consumer incomes

    (B) A decrease in the price of motorcycles

    (C) An increase in the price of bicycles

    (D) An increase in people's tastes and preferences for motorcycles

5. "Rising oil prices have caused a sharp decrease in the demand for oil." Speaking precisely, and using terms as they are defined by economists, choose the statement that best describes this quotation.

    (A) The quotation is correct: an increase in price causes a decrease in demand.

    (B) The quotation is incorrect: an increase in price causes an increase in demand, not a decrease in demand.

    (C) The quotation is incorrect: an increase in price causes a decrease in the quantity demanded, not a decrease in demand.

    (D) The quotation is incorrect: an increase in price causes an increase in the quantity demanded, not a decrease in demand.

6. "As the price of domestic automobiles has risen, customers have found foreign autos to be a better bargain. Consequently, domestic auto sales have been decreasing, and foreign auto sales have been increasing." Using only the information in this quotation and assuming everything else remains constant, which of the following best describes this statement?

    (A) A shift in the demand curves for both domestic and foreign automobiles

    (B) A movement along the demand curves for both foreign and domestic automobiles

    (C) A movement along the demand curve for domestic autos, and a shift in the demand curve for foreign autos

    (D) A shift in the demand curve for domestic autos, and a movement along the demand curve for foreign autos

Reasons for Changes in Demand

Part A: Does the Demand Curve Shift?

Read the eight newspaper headlines in Table 1-5.1, and use the table to record the impact of each event on the demand for U.S.-made autos. In the second column, indicate whether the event in the headline will cause consumers to buy more or less U.S.-made autos. Use the third column to indicate whether there is a change in demand (ΔD) or a change in quantity demanded (ΔQd) for U.S.-made autos. In the third column, decide whether the demand curve shifts to the right or left or does not shift. Finally, indicate the letter for the new demand curve. Use Figure 1-5.1 to help you. **Always start at curve B**, and move only one curve at a time.

Table 1-5.1
Impact of Events on Demand for U.S.-Made Autos

Headline	Will consumers buy more or less U.S. autos?	Is there a change in demand (ΔD) or a change in quantity demanded (ΔQd)?	Does the demand curve for U.S. autos shift to the right or left or not shift?	What is the new demand curve for U.S. autos?
1. Consumers' Income Drops	More / Less	ΔD / ΔQd	Right / Left / No Shift	A / B / C
2. Millions of Immigrants Enter the U.S.	More / Less	ΔD / ΔQd	Right / Left / No Shift	A / B / C
3. Price of Foreign Autos Drop	More / Less	ΔD / ΔQd	Right / Left / No Shift	A / B / C
4. Major Cities Add Inexpensive Bus Lines	More / Less	ΔD / ΔQd	Right / Left / No Shift	A / B / C
5. Price of U.S. Autos Rises	More / Less	ΔD / ΔQd	Right / Left / No Shift	A / B / C
6. Price of U.S. Autos Expected to Rise Soon	More / Less	ΔD / Qd	Right / Left / No Shift	A / B / C
7. Families Look Forward to Summer Vacations	More / Less	ΔD / ΔQd	Right / Left / No Shift	A / B / C
8. U.S. Auto Firms Launch Effective Ad Campaigns	More / Less	ΔD / ΔQd	Right / Left / No Shift	A / B / C

Figure 1-5.1
Demand for U.S.-Made Autos

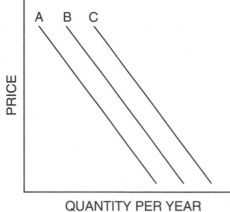

Part B: Why Does the Demand Curve Shift?

Categorize each change in demand in Part A according to the reason why demand changed. A given demand curve assumes that consumer expectations, consumer tastes, the number of consumers in the market, the income of consumers, and the prices of substitutes and complements are unchanged. In Table 1-5.2, place an X next to the reason that the event described in the headline caused a change in demand. One headline will have no answer because it will result in a change in quantity demanded rather than a change in demand.

Table 1-5.2
Reasons for a Change in Demand for U.S.-Made Autos

Reason	Headline number							
	1	2	3	4	5	6	7	8
9. A change in consumer expectations								
10. A change in consumer tastes								
11. A change in the number of consumer in the market								
12. A change in income								
13. A change in the price of a substitute good								
14. A change in the price of a complementary good								

Supply Curves, Movements along Supply Curves, and Shifts in Supply Curves

In this activity, we will assume that the supply curve of Greebes is upward sloping.

Part A: A Change in Supply versus a Change in Quantity Supplied

Student Alert: The distinction between a "change in supply" and a "change in quantity supplied" is very important!

Study the data in Table 1-6.1 and plot the supply of Greebes on the graph in Figure 1-6.1. Label the supply curve S and answer the questions that follow.

Table 1-6.1
Supply of Greebes

Price (per Greebe)	Quantity supplied per week (millions of Greebes)
$0.05	0
$0.10	50
$0.15	100
$0.20	150
$0.25	200
$0.30	250
$0.35	300
$0.40	350

Figure 1-6.1
Supply of Greebes

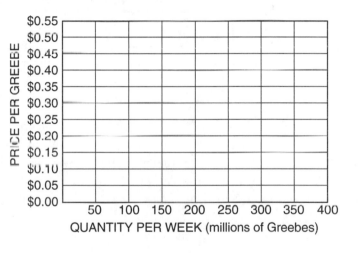

1. The data for supply curve S indicate that at a price of $0.25 per Greebe, suppliers would be willing to offer _____ million Greebes. All other things held constant, if the price of Greebes increased to $0.30 per Greebe, suppliers would be willing to offer _____ million Greebes. Such a change would be an increase in (*supply / quantity supplied*). All other things held things constant, if the price of Greebes decreased to $0.20 per Greebe, suppliers would be willing to offer _____ million Greebes. Such a change would be called a decrease in (*supply / quantity supplied*).

Now, let's suppose that there is a change in the price of several of the raw materials used in making Greebes. This change in the *ceteris paribus* conditions underlying the original supply of Greebes will result in a new set of data, such as that shown in Table 1-6.2. Study the data, and plot this supply of Greebes on the graph in Figure 1-6.1. Label the new supply curve S_1 and answer the questions that follow.

Table 1-6.2
New Supply of Greebes

Price (per Greebe)	Quantity supplied per week (millions of Greebes)
$0.15	0
$0.20	50
$0.25	100
$0.30	150
$0.35	200
$0.40	250

2. Comparing the new supply curve (S_1) with the original supply curve (S), we can say that the change in the supply of Greebes results in a shift of the supply curve to the (*left / right*). Such a shift indicates that at each of the possible prices shown, suppliers are now willing to offer a (*smaller / larger*) quantity; and at each of the possible quantities shown, suppliers are willing to accept a (*higher / lower*) minimum price. The cause of this supply curve shift was a(n) (*increase / decrease*) in prices of several of the raw materials used in making Greebes.

Now, let's suppose that there is a dramatic change in the price of Silopanna, a resource used in the production of Greebes. This change in the *ceteris paribus* conditions underlying the original supply of Greebes will result in a new set of data shown in Table 1-6.3. Study the data, and plot this supply of Greebes on the graph in Figure 1-6.1. Label the new supply curve S_2 and answer the questions that follow.

Table 1-6.3
New Supply of Greebes

Price (per Greebe)	Quantity supplied per week (millions of Greebes)
$0.10	150
$0.15	200
$0.20	250
$0.25	300
$0.30	350
$0.35	400

3. Comparing the new supply curve (S_2) with the original supply curve (S), we can say that the change in the supply of Greebes results in a shift of the supply curve to the (*left / right*). Such a shift indicates that at each of the possible prices shown, suppliers are now willing to offer a (*smaller / larger*) quantity; and at each of the possible quantities shown, suppliers are willing to accept a (*lower / higher*) minimum price. The cause of this supply curve shift is a(n) (*increase / decrease*) in the price of Silopanna, a resource used in the production of Greebes.

Part B: Do You Get It?

Now, to check your understanding, choose the answer you think is the one best alternative in each of the following multiple-choice questions.

4. All other things held constant, which of the following would *not* cause a change in the supply of beef?

   (A) A decrease in the price of beef

   (B) A decrease in the price of cattle feed

   (C) An increase in the price of cattle feed

   (D) An increase in the cost of transporting cattle to market

5. "Falling oil prices have caused a sharp decrease in the supply of oil." Speaking precisely, and using terms as they are defined by economists, choose the statement that best describes this quotation.

(A) The quotation is correct: a decrease in price causes a decrease in supply.

(B) The quotation is incorrect: a decrease in price causes an increase in supply, not a decrease in supply.

(C) The quotation is incorrect: a decrease in price causes an increase in the quantity supplied, not a decrease in supply.

(D) The quotation is incorrect: a decrease in price causes a decrease in the quantity supplied, not a decrease in supply.

6. You overhear a fellow student say, "Economic markets are confusing. If supply increases, then price decreases; but if price decreases, then supply also will decrease. If supply falls, price will rise; but if price rises, supply also will rise." Dispel your friend's obvious confusion (in no more than one short paragraph) below.

Reasons for Changes in Supply

Part A: Does the Supply Curve Shift?

Read the eight newspaper headlines in Table 1-7.1, and use the table to record the impact of each event on the supply of cars from U.S. auto producers. In the second column, indicate whether the event in the headline will cause American auto producers to provide more or less cars. Use the third column to indicate whether there is a change in supply (ΔS) or a change in quantity supplied (ΔQs) of cars. In the third column, decide whether the supply curve shifts to the right or left or does not shift. Finally, indicate the letter for the new supply curve. Use Figure 1-7.1 to help you. **Always start at curve B**, and move only one curve at a time.

 Table 1-7.1
Impact of Events on Supply of U.S.-Made Autos

Headline	Should U.S. auto firms produce more or less?	Is there a change in supply (ΔS) or a change in quantity supplied (ΔQs)?	Does the supply curve of cars shift to the right or left or not shift?	What is the new supply curve for cars?
1. Auto Workers' Union Agrees to Wage Cuts	More / Less	ΔS / ΔQs	Right / Left / No Shift	A / B / C
2. New Robot Technology Increases Efficiency	More / Less	ΔS / ΔQs	Right / Left / No Shift	A / B / C
3. Price of U.S. Cars Increases	More / Less	ΔS / ΔQs	Right / Left / No Shift	A / B / C
4. Nationwide Auto Workers Strike Begins	More / Less	ΔS / ΔQs	Right / Left / No Shift	A / B / C
5. Cost of Steel Decreases	More / Less	ΔS / ΔQs	Right / Left / No Shift	A / B / C
6. Major Auto Producer Goes Out of Business	More / Less	ΔS / ΔQs	Right / Left / No Shift	A / B / C
7. Buyers Reject New Car Models	More / Less	ΔS / ΔQs	Right / Left / No Shift	A / B / C
8. Government Gives Car Producers a Subsidy	More / Less	ΔS / ΔQs	Right / Left / No Shift	A / B / C

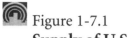 Figure 1-7.1
Supply of U.S.-Made Cars

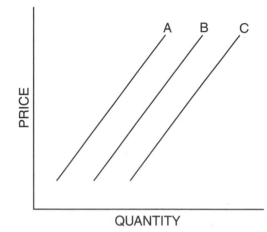

Part B: Why Does the Supply Curve Shift?

Categorize each change in supply in Part A according to the reason why supply changed. In Table 1-7.2, place an X next to the reason that the headline indicated a change in supply. In some cases, more than one headline could be matched to a reason. It is possible a headline does not indicate a shift in supply because it will result in a change in quantity supplied rather than a change in supply.

 Table 1-7.2
Impact of Events on Supply of U.S.-Made Autos

	Headline number							
Reason	1	2	3	4	5	6	7	8
9. A change in costs of inputs to production process								
10. A change in technology								
11. A change in the number of producers in the market								
12. Government policies								

Equilibrium Price and Equilibrium Quantity

Table 1-8.1 below shows the demand for Greebes and the supply of Greebes. Plot these data on the axes in Figure 1-8.1. Label the demand curve D and label the supply curve S. Then answer the questions that follow.

 *Student Alert:* A "change in demand" or a "change in supply" results in a change in price, while a "change in quantity demanded" or a "change in quantity supplied" is the result of a change in price.

 Table 1-8.1
Demand for and Supply of Greebes

Price (per Greebe)	Quantity demanded (millions of Greebes)	Quantity supplied (millions of Greebes)
$0.05	400	0
$0.10	350	50
$0.15	300	100
$0.20	250	150
$0.25	200	200
$0.30	150	250
$0.35	100	300
$0.40	50	350
$0.45	0	400

Figure 1-8.1
Demand for and Supply of Greebes

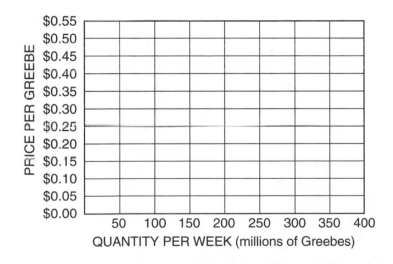

1. Under these conditions, competitive market forces would tend to establish an equilibrium price of _____ per Greebe and an equilibrium quantity of _____ million Greebes.

2. If the price currently prevailing in the market is $0.30 per Greebe, buyers would want to buy _____ million Greebes and sellers would want to sell _____ million Greebes. Under these conditions, there would be a (*shortage / surplus*) of _____ million Greebes. Competitive market forces would cause the price to (*increase / decrease*) to a price of _____ per Greebe. At this new price, buyers would now want to buy _____ million Greebes, and sellers now want to sell _____ million Greebes. Because of this change in (*price / underlying conditions*), the (*demand / quantity demanded*) (*increased / decreased*) by _____ million Greebes, and the (*supply / quantity supplied*) (*increased / decreased*) by _____ million Greebes.

3. If the price currently prevailing in the market is $0.20 per Greebe, buyers would want to buy _____ million Greebes, and sellers would want to sell _____ million Greebes. Under these conditions, there would be a (*shortage / surplus*) of _____ million Greebes. Competitive market forces would cause the price to (*increase / decrease*) to a price of _____ per Greebe. At this new price, buyers would now want to buy _____ million Greebes, and sellers now want to sell _____ million Greebes. Because of this change in (*price / underlying conditions*), the (*demand / quantity demanded*) (*increased / decreased*) by _____ million Greebes, and the (*supply / quantity supplied*) (*increased / decreased*) by _____ million Greebes.

4. At equilibrium, is each of the following true or false? Explain.

   (A) The quantity demanded is equal to the quantity supplied.

   (B) Demand equals supply.

5. Now, suppose a mysterious blight causes the supply schedule for Greebes to change as shown in Table 1-8.2:

 Table 1-8.2
New Supply of Greebes

Price (per Greebe)	Quantity supplied (millions of Greebes)
$0.15	0
$0.20	50
$0.25	100
$0.30	150
$0.35	200

Plot the new supply schedule on the axes in Figure 1-8.1 and label it S_1. Label the new equilibrium E_1. Under these conditions, competitive market forces would establish an equilibrium price of _____ per Greebe and an equilibrium quantity of _____ million Greebes.

Compared with the equilibrium price in Question 1, we say that because of this change in (*price / underlying conditions*), the (*supply / quantity supplied*) changed; and both the equilibrium price and the equilibrium quantity changed. The equilibrium price (*increased / decreased*), and the equilibrium quantity (*increased / decreased*).

Compared with the consumer and producer surpluses in Question 4, consumer surplus has (*increased / decreased*), and producer surplus has (*increased / decreased*).

6. Now, with the supply schedule at S_1, suppose further that a sharp drop in people's incomes as the result of a prolonged recession causes the demand schedule to change as shown in Table 1-8.3:

Table 1-8.3
New Demand for Greebes

Price (per Greebe)	Quantity demanded (millions of Greebes)
$0.15	200
$0.20	150
$0.25	100
$0.30	50

Plot the new demand schedule on the axes in Figure 1-8.1 and label it D_1. Label the new equilibrium E_2. Under these conditions, with the supply schedule at S_1, competitive market forces would establish an equilibrium price of _____ per Greebe and an equilibrium quantity of _____ million Greebes. Compared with the equilibrium price in Question 5, because of this change in (*price / underlying conditions*), the (*demand / quantity demanded*) changed. The equilibrium price (*increased / decreased*), and the equilibrium quantity (*increased / decreased*).

Shifts in Supply and Demand

Part A: The Market for Jelly Beans

Fill in the blanks with the letter of the graph that illustrates each situation. You may use a graph more than once.

Figure 1-9.1
The Supply and Demand for Jelly Beans

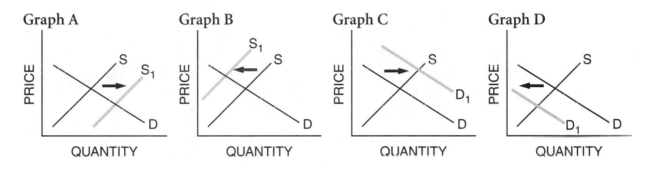

1. The price of sugar, a key ingredient in producing jelly beans, increases. _____

2. The price of bubble gum, a close substitute for jelly beans, increases. _____

3. A machine is invented that makes jelly beans at a lower cost. _____

4. The government places a tax on foreign jelly beans, which have a considerable share of the market. _____

5. The price of soda, a complementary good for jelly beans, increases. _____

6. Widespread prosperity allows people to buy more jelly beans. _____

Part B: Apples, Pears, and Pies

Connecticut ships large amounts of apples to all parts of the United States by rail. Circle the words that show the effects on price and quantity for each situation, and complete the graphs below, showing how a hurricane that destroys apples before they are picked in Connecticut might affect the price and quantity of each commodity. Then provide your reasoning.

7. **Apples in Boston**

   Price: *Rises / Unchanged / Falls*

   Quantity: *Rises / Unchanged / Falls*

   Reason:

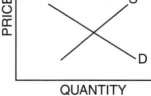

8. **Land devoted to apple orchards in the state of Washington**

   Price: *Rises / Unchanged / Falls*

   Quantity: *Rises / Unchanged / Falls*

   Reason:

9. **Apples grown in the state of Washington**

   Price: *Rises / Unchanged / Falls*

   Quantity: *Rises / Unchanged / Falls*

   Reason:

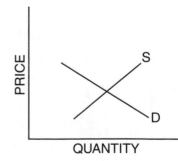

10. **Pears**

    Price: *Rises / Unchanged / Falls*

    Quantity: *Rises / Unchanged / Falls*

    Reason:

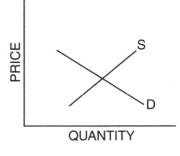

11. **Apple pies**

    Price: *Rises / Unchanged / Falls*

    Quantity: *Rises / Unchanged / Falls*

    Reason:

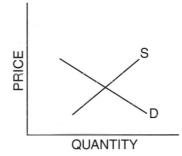

The Business Cycle: Introduction to Macroeconomic Indicators

Overview

The 1930s were marked by periods of chronically high unemployment in the United States. After World War II, Congress passed the Employment Act of 1946, which stated that it was the policy and responsibility of the federal government to use all practical means to promote maximum employment, production, and purchasing power. The Employment Act of 1946 established three important goals for the economy:

1. *Full employment* exists when most individuals who are willing and able to work at the prevailing wages in the economy are employed. Even under conditions of full employment, there will be some temporary unemployment as workers change jobs and as new workers seek their first jobs.

2. *Price stability* exists when the average level of prices in the economy is neither increasing nor decreasing. The goal of price stability does not imply that prices of individual items should not change—only that the average level of prices should not change.

3. *Economic growth* exists when the economy produces increasing amounts of goods and services over the long term. If the increase is greater than the increase in population, the amount of goods and services available per person will rise, and thus the nation's standard of living will improve.

Measuring the Achievement of Economic Goals

To determine how well we are achieving economic goals requires measuring the levels of employment, prices, and economic growth.

Measuring Employment

The civilian *unemployment rate* measures how well we are achieving the goal of full employment. The unemployment rate is derived from a national survey of about 60,000 households. Each month the federal government asks the households about the employment status of household members aged 16 and older (the adult population). The survey puts each person in one of three categories: employed, unemployed, or not in the labor force. People who are at work (the employed) plus those who are not working but are willing and able to work and are actively looking for work (the unemployed) make up the *labor force*. The labor force is much smaller than the total adult population because many individuals are not willing or able to work.

Measuring Price Changes

A *price index* measures price changes in the economy. By using a price index, you can combine the prices of a number of goods and/or services and express in one number the average change for all the prices. The consumer price index, or CPI, is the measure of price changes that is probably most familiar to people. It measures changes in the prices of goods and services commonly bought by consumers.

Measuring Short-Run Economic Growth

To measure fluctuations in output (short-run economic growth), we measure increases in the quantity of goods and services produced in the economy from quarter to quarter or year to year. The *gross domestic product*, or GDP, is commonly used to measure economic growth. The GDP is the dollar value at market prices of all final goods and services produced in the economy during a stated period. Real GDP is the GDP adjusted for changes in the price of goods.

The Business Cycle

The *business cycle* refers to the ups and downs in an economy. In the short run, the economy alternates between upturns and downturns as measured by the three macroeconomic indicators. Figure 1-10.1 shows a graph of the business cycle.

Figure 1-10.1
The Business Cycle

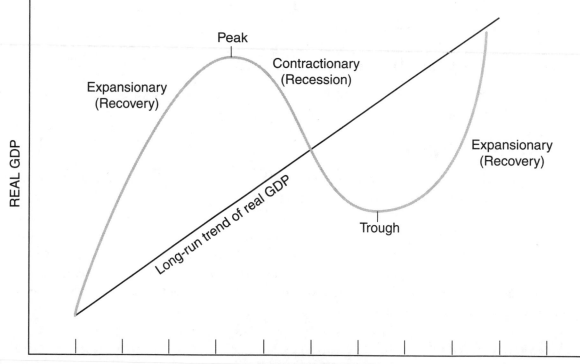

The curved line on Figure 1-10.1 shows a sample business cycle for an economy. The straight line represents the long-run trend of real GDP.

The business cycle can be divided into four phases:

1. *Expansionary*. Real output in the economy is increasing and the unemployment rate is declining. As the economic expansion continues, inflation may begin to accelerate. The early part of an expansionary phase is also called a recovery phase.

2. *Peak*. Real output, GDP, is at its highest point of the business cycle.

3. *Contractionary*. Real output in the economy is decreasing, and the unemployment rate is rising. As the contraction continues, inflationary pressures subside. The later stage of a contractionary phase is also called a recession.

4. *Trough*. The lowest point of real GDP reached during the business cycle is known as the trough. If the trough is particularly deep, it may be called a depression. A depression is an economic situation where the level of output falls to especially low levels and unemployment climbs to very high levels. There is no precise decline in output at which a serious recession becomes a depression. However, most business cycles do not end in a depression.

Draw a graph of a business cycle using unemployment as your measure of economic activity. That is, label the vertical axis with the unemployment rate. Make sure that you also label the horizontal axis. Label the phases of the business cycle on your graph. Remember that you are graphing the unemployment rate (rather than output) on your graph. Think about what happens to the unemployment rate during each phase of the business cycle!

On your graph, plot a point indicating where in the business cycle you think the economy is currently operating. Explain how you selected that location.

Circle the letter of each correct answer.

1. The crucial problem of economics is
   (A) establishing a fair tax system.
   (B) providing social goods and services.
   (C) developing a price mechanism that reflects the relative scarcities of products and resources.
   (D) allocating scarce productive resources to satisfy unlimited wants.
   (E) enacting a set of laws that protects resources from overuse.

2. When one decision is made, the next best alternative not selected is called
   (A) economic resource.
   (B) opportunity cost.
   (C) scarcity.
   (D) comparative disadvantage.
   (E) production.

3. Which of the following is true if the production possibilities curve is a curved line concave to the origin?
   (A) Resources are perfectly substitutable between the production of the two goods.
   (B) It is possible to produce more of both products.
   (C) Both products are equally capable of satisfying consumer wants.
   (D) The prices of the two products are the same.
   (E) As more of one good is produced, increasing amounts of the other good must be given up.

4. Which of the following will *not* change the demand for oranges?
   (A) A change in consumers' incomes
   (B) A change in the price of grapefruits, a substitute for oranges
   (C) A change in the price of oranges
   (D) A change in consumers' taste for oranges
   (E) An expectation that the price of oranges will change in the future

5. To be considered scarce, an economic resource must be
   (A) limited but not free or desirable.
   (B) limited and free, but not desirable.
   (C) limited and desirable, but not free.
   (D) limited, free, and desirable.
   (E) free and desirable, but not limited.

6. If there is an increase in demand for a good, what will most likely happen to the price and quantity of the good exchanged?

	Price	Quantity
(A)	No change	No change
(B)	Increase	Increase
(C)	Increase	Decrease
(D)	Decrease	Increase
(E)	Decrease	Decrease

7. Which of the following goods would be considered scarce?
   (A) Education
   (B) Gold
   (C) Time
   (D) Education and gold
   (E) Education, gold, and time

8. An increase in the price of gasoline will cause the demand curve for tires to shift in which direction?

   (A) To the left, because gasoline and tires are substitutes

   (B) To the left, because gasoline and tires are complements

   (C) To the right, because gasoline and tires are substitutes

   (D) To the right, because gasoline and tires are complements

   (E) To the right, because an increase in the price of gasoline makes consumers poorer and thus not willing to pay as much for tires

9. Which of the following indicates that the macroeconomy is achieving its economic goals?

   (A) Deflation

   (B) Inflation

   (C) Economic growth

   (D) Unemplyoment

   (E) Declining GDP

10. In which way does a straight-line production possibilities curve differ from a concave production possibilities curve?

    (A) A straight-line production possibilities curve has a decreasing opportunity cost.

    (B) A straight-line production possibilities curve has a constant opportunity cost.

    (C) A straight-line production possibilities curve has an increasing opportunity cost.

    (D) A straight-line production possibilities curve does not show opportunity cost.

    (E) There is no difference between the two production possibilities curves.

11. The law of increasing opportunity cost is reflected in the shape of the

    (A) production possibilities curve concave to the origin.

    (B) production possibilities curve convex to the origin.

    (C) horizontal production possibilities curve.

    (D) straight-line production possibilities curve.

    (E) upward-sloping production possibilities curve.

The figure below is used for questions 12 through 15. It shows the production possibilities curve for a country with full employment of a given-size labor force.

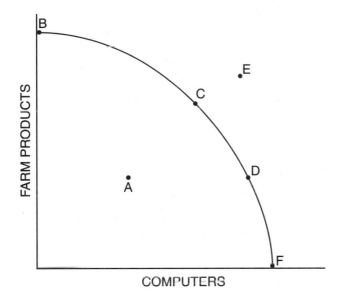

12. If the country is currently producing at Point C, it can produce more computers by doing which of the following?

(A) Moving to Point A

(B) Moving to Point B

(C) Moving to Point D

(D) Moving to Point E

(E) Remaining at Point C

13. Which of the following statements about the production possibilities curve is true?

(A) Point A is not attainable in a developed society.

(B) Point D is not attainable given the society's resources.

(C) The relative position of Points C and D reflect production alternatives rather than relative prices.

(D) Elimination of unemployment will move the production possibilities curve to the right, closer to Point E.

(E) Point E lies outside the production possibilities curve because it represents a combination of resources not desired by the citizens of the country.

14. How might Point E be attained?

(A) If the country's resources were more fully employed

(B) If the country's resources were shifted to encourage more efficient use of scarce resources

(C) If improvements in technology occurred in either the computer sector or the farm products sector

(D) If firms decreased their output of computers

(E) If the nation used more of its scarce resources to produce farm products

15. The production possibilities curve of the country would be most likely to shift to the right if the country were currently producing at which of the following points?

(A) Point A

(B) Point B

(C) Point C

(D) Point D

(E) Point E

The figure below is used for questions 16, 17, and 18. It shows the production possibilities curve for two types of goods for a country with full employment of a given-size labor force.

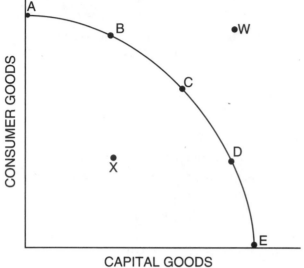

16. If the country is currently producing at Point C, it can produce more capital goods by moving in the direction of

    (A) Point A.

    (B) Point B.

    (C) Point D.

    (D) Point W.

    (E) Point X.

17. If the country moves from Point C to Point D, future economic growth will

    (A) decrease.

    (B) increase.

    (C) not change, but consumer satisfaction will increase.

    (D) not change, but unemployment will increase.

    (E) not change, but inflation will increase.

18. Which of the following is most likely to cause the production possibilities curve to shift outward toward Point W?

    (A) Employing the country's resources more fully

    (B) Shifting the country's resources to encourage more efficient use of scarce resources

    (C) Improving the technology for the production of either consumer or capital goods

    (D) Decreasing production of capital goods

    (E) Shifting some scarce resources to produce consumer goods in the current period

19. The opportunity cost of producing an additional unit of product J is

    (A) the dollar value of resources used to make the extra unit of product J.

    (B) the retail price paid for product J.

    (C) the wholesale price of product J.

    (D) the amount of product K that could have been produced with the resources used to make the unit of J.

    (E) the profit that was earned from producing product J.

20. Which of the following would cause a leftward shift of the production possibilities curve?

    (A) An increase in unemployment

    (B) An increase in inflation

    (C) An increase in capital equipment

    (D) A decrease in consumer demand

    (E) A decrease in working-age population

21. Which of the following would cause an outward or rightward shift in the production possibilities curve?

    (A) An increase in unemployment

    (B) An increase in inflation

    (C) An increase in capital equipment

    (D) A decrease in natural resources

    (E) A decrease in the number of workers

Use the following table for questions 22, 23, and 24.

Mars		Venus	
Food	Clothing	Food	Clothing
0	30	0	40
2	24	4	32
4	18	8*	24*
6*	12*	12	16
8	6	16	8
10	0	20	0

Two nations, Mars and Venus, each produce food and clothing. The table above gives points on each nation's production possibilities curve. The asterisks indicate their current point of production.

22. In Mars, the opportunity cost of obtaining the first two units of food is how many units of clothing?

   (A) 2   (D) 8

   (B) 3   (E) 12

   (C) 6

23. In Venus, the opportunity cost of the first unit of

   (A) food is two units of clothing.

   (B) food is eight units of clothing.

   (C) clothing is two units of food.

   (D) clothing is four units of food.

   (E) clothing is eight units of food.

24. Which of the following statements is correct based on the concept of comparative advantage?

   (A) Mars and Venus should continue producing the quantities indicated by the asterisks.

   (B) Mars should specialize in the production of food.

   (C) Mars should specialize in the production of clothing.

   (D) Venus has the comparative advantage in clothing.

   (E) Mars has an absolute advantage in the production of food.

25. The table below shows the number of hours needed to produce one bushel of soybeans and one bushel of rice in each of two countries.

Country	One bushel of soybeans	One bushel of rice
U.S.	5 hours	7 hours
Japan	15 hours	10 hours

Which of the following statements must be true?

   (A) The U.S. has both the absolute and comparative advantage in producing soybeans.

   (B) Japan has both the absolute and comparative advantage in producing soybeans.

   (C) The U.S. has both the absolute and comparative advantage in producing rice.

   (D) Japan has both the absolute and comparative advantage in producing rice.

   (E) Japan has the absolute advantage in producing soybeans and the comparative advantage in producing rice.

26. According to the theory of comparative advantage, a good should be produced where

   (A) its explicit costs are least.

   (B) its opportunity costs are least.

   (C) the cost of real resources used is least.

   (D) production can occur with the greatest increase in employment.

   (E) production can occur with the least increase in employment.

27. Which of the following is at its highest at the trough of a business cycle?

   (A) Employment

   (B) Inflation

   (C) Economic growth

   (D) Unemployment

   (E) Gross domestic product

28. If GDP is declining, the economy is most likely in which phase of the business cycle?

    (A) Recovery

    (B) Expansionary

    (C) Trough

    (D) Contractionary

    (E) Peak

29. Which of the following will *not* cause the demand curve for athletic shoes to shift?

    (A) A change in tastes for athletic shoes

    (B) Widespread advertising campaign for athletic shoes

    (C) Increase in money incomes of athletic-shoe consumers

    (D) Expectations that the price of athletic shoes will decrease in the future

    (E) A decrease in the price of athletic shoes

30. Assume that the demand for apples is downward sloping. If the price of apples falls from $0.80 per pound to $0.65 per pound, which of the following will occur?

    (A) A smaller quantity of apples will be demanded.

    (B) A larger quantity of apples will be demanded.

    (C) Demand for apples will decrease.

    (D) Demand for apples will increase.

    (E) Supply of apples will decrease.

MACROECONOMICS

Measuring Economic Performance

Unit 2

■ Macroeconomics is the study of the economy as a whole; microeconomics is the study of individual parts of the economy such as businesses, households, and prices. Macroeconomics looks at the forest while microeconomics looks at the trees.

■ A circular flow diagram illustrates the major flows of goods and services, resources, and income in an economy. It shows how changes in these flows can alter the level of goods and services, employment, and income.

■ Gross domestic product (GDP) is the market value of all final goods and services produced in a nation in one year. It is the most important measure of production and output.

■ GDP may be calculated two ways:

1. **The expenditures approach:** add all the consumption, investment, government expenditures, and net exports

   GDP = C + I + G + Xn.

2. **The income approach:** add all the income received by owners of resources (land, labor, capital, entrepreneurship) in the economy.

   National income = wages + rent + interest + profit.

■ The expenditures approach to calculating GDP counts only final goods and services to avoid double counting. That is, it does not count intermediate goods and services.

■ The expenditures approach to calculating GDP does not count the purchase of secondhand goods, stocks and bonds, or items not purchased in a legal market because these do not represent new production during the year.

■ The income approach to calculating GDP includes profits and income earned by

foreigners in the United States but does not count income and profits earned by U.S. citizens abroad, transfer payments like Social Security, unemployment compensation, or certain interest payments.

■ Inflation is a general increase in the price level in the economy. Savers, lenders, and people on fixed incomes generally are hurt by unanticipated inflation. Borrowers gain from unanticipated inflation.

■ Price indices measure price changes in the economy. They are used to compare the prices of a given bundle or "market basket" of goods and services in one year with the prices of the same bundle/market basket in another year.

■ The most frequently used price indices are the GDP price deflator, the Consumer Price Index (CPI), and the Producer Price Index (PPI).

■ Price changes over time are measured by comparing prices each year to the prices in a selected year, called the base year. The price level in the base year has an index number of 100. The price level in other years is expressed in relation to the price level in the base year.

$$\text{Price index} = \frac{\text{current-year price of a market basket}}{\text{base-year price of a market basket}} \times 100.$$

■ If domestic prices increase relative to prices in other countries, imports will increase while exports decrease because people want to purchase the goods and services where they are relatively cheaper.

■ The labor force is defined as people who have a job (employed) and people who are not working but are actively seeking a job (unemployed). The labor force participation rate is the percentage of the population over the age of 16 that is in the labor force.

■ Unemployment occurs when people who are willing and able to work are not working. The unemployment rate equals the number of people who are not working but who are actively seeking a job as a percentage of the labor force.

■ There are three types of unemployment: frictional, cyclical, and structural.

■ The unemployment rate associated with full employment is above zero because frictional and structural unemployment will always exist. Full employment occurs where cyclical unemployment equals zero.

■ The unemployment rate at full employment is called the natural rate of unemployment.

Understanding the Circular Flow of the Macroeconomy

Firms provide goods and services to households through the product market. Households pay firms for these goods and services.

Households supply firms with the factors of production (also called resources) through the factor market. Firms pay households for resources (land, labor, capital, and entrepreneurial skill).

The income firms pay to households includes rent, wages, interest, and profits. It equals the dollar value of the output sold as shown in the circular flow diagram in Figure 2-1.1. The flow on the diagram that includes expenditures for goods and services produced and sold in the product market represents gross domestic product (GDP). The approach to measuring GDP using this flow is called the *expenditures approach*.

🛈 *Student Alert:* Using the expenditures approach,

$$GDP = C + I + G + Xn.$$

The details about this equation for GDP are developed in a later activity. For now, make sure you understand how the expenditures approach measures GDP, and that this equation forms the basis for models developed throughout the rest of the course.

The flow on the diagram that includes payments for the resources used to produce goods and services in the factor market is another way to represent GDP. The approach to measuring GDP using this flow is called the *income approach*.

In addition to the basic flow of economic activity illustrated by the flows between the product and factor markets shown on the outside of the diagram, there are leakages from the flow and injections into the flow that affect its size. The leakages and injections happen through the government, financial institutions (e.g., banks), and international trade. These are shown using the boxes in the center of the circular flow diagram.

Identify which of the following terms belongs in each of the numbered blanks in the circular flow diagram, and fill in the blanks.

Expenditure approach

Income approach

Taxes

Saving

Investment

Exports

Government spending

Imports

Payments for resources (rent/wages/interest/profit)

Payments for goods and services

Income (rent/wages/interest/profit)

Revenue from selling goods and services

 Figure 2-1.1

The Circular Flow of Resources, Goods, Services, and Money Payments

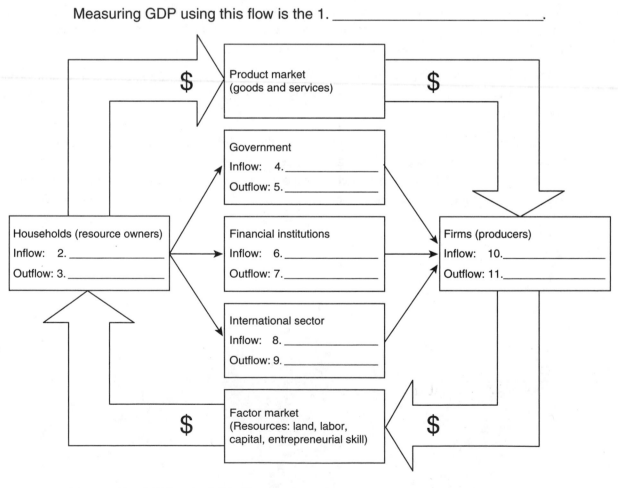

Measuring GDP using this flow is the 1. _____.

Product market (goods and services)

Government
Inflow: 4. _____
Outflow: 5. _____

Households (resource owners)
Inflow: 2. _____
Outflow: 3. _____

Financial institutions
Inflow: 6. _____
Outflow: 7. _____

Firms (producers)
Inflow: 10. _____
Outflow: 11. _____

International sector
Inflow: 8. _____
Outflow: 9. _____

Factor market (Resources: land, labor, capital, entrepreneurial skill)

Measuring GDP using this flow is the 12. _____.

Gross Domestic Product

Measuring Short-Run Economic Growth

Fluctuations in output are measured by increases or decreases in the quantity of goods and services produced in the economy over time. The *gross domestic product*, or GDP, is commonly used to measure economic growth. The GDP is the dollar value of all *final* goods and services produced in the economy during a stated period.

Final goods are goods intended for consumers. For example, gasoline is a final good purchased by consumers but crude oil, used to make gasoline, is not.

Note that GDP does not count the purchase of secondhand goods or stocks and bonds because these do not represent new production during the year. GDP also does not include items that are not exchanged in a legal market (e.g., mowing your own lawn, caring for your own children, or purchasing illegal goods).

Is This Counted as Part of GDP?

Determine if each of the following is included or excluded when calculating GDP. Briefly explain why.

1. A monthly check received by an economics student who has been granted a government scholarship *excluded transfer payment*

2. A farmer's purchase of a new tractor *included investment spending*

3. A plumber's purchase of a two-year-old used truck *excluded*

4. Cashing a U.S. government bond *excluded financial asset*

5. The services of a barber cutting his own hair *excluded non-market activity*

6. A Social Security check from the government to a retired store clerk *excluded transfer payment*

7. Chevrolet's purchase of tires to put on the cars they are producing *excluded intermediate good*

8. The government's purchase of a new submarine for the Navy *included gov. spending*

9. A barber's income from cutting hair *included service(good)*

10. Income received from the sale of Nike stock *excluded financial*

GDP: Is It Counted and Where?

For each of the following items, write one of the following in the space provided:

        C if the item is counted as *consumption spending.*
        I if the item is counted as *investment spending.*
        G if the item is counted as *government spending.*
        Xn if the item is counted as *net exports.*
        NC if the item is *not counted* in GDP.

_C_ 11. You spend $10.00 to see a movie.

_I/C_ 12. A family pays a contractor $150,000 for a house he built for them this year.

_NC_ 13. A family pays $75,000 for a house built three years ago. *Second hand sale*

_C_ 14. An accountant pays a tailor $175 to sew a suit for her.

_G_ 15. The government increases its defense expenditures by $1,000,000,000.

_NC_ 16. The government makes a $300 Social Security payment to a retired person. *transfer payment*

_NC_ 17. You buy McDonald's stock for $1,000 in the stock market. *financial transaction*

_I_ 18. At the end of a year, a flour-milling firm finds that its inventories of grain and flour are $10,000 higher than its inventories at the beginning of the year.

_NC_ 19. Parents work hard caring for their two children.

_I_ 20. Ford Motor Company buys new auto-making robots.

_C_ 21. You pay $800 a month to rent an apartment.

_I_ 22. Consumer electronics corporation Apple Inc. builds a new factory in the United States.

_NC_ 23. R.J. Reynolds buys control of Nabisco. *finacial transaction*

_Xn_ 24. You buy a new Toyota that was made in Japan.

_C_ 25. You pay tuition to attend college.

Inflation

Inflation is an overall increase in the price level in an economy. *Deflation* is the opposite of inflation. Deflation is an overall decrease in the price level. A change in the price of just one or a few goods does not constitute inflation or deflation. After the price level increases, a dollar will buy less than it would before. When there is going to be inflation, people are better off buying now, before prices go up. After the price level falls, a dollar will buy more than it would before. When there is going to be deflation, people are better off waiting to buy later, when prices go down.

If people anticipate inflation, they will build that expectation into their decisions. For example, workers will demand higher wages to keep their purchasing power the same if prices are expected to rise. Then, when inflation leads to higher prices, workers are not hurt or helped because their higher wages allow them to purchase the same amount of goods and services. However, when inflation is *unanticipated*, people do not build it into their decisions, and some people are hurt while others are helped. For example, when there is unanticipated inflation, borrowers are helped while lenders are hurt. People who borrow money receive a loan before prices rise, when the money will buy more. However, they pay the money back later, after prices rise, when the money won't buy as much. With inflation, the borrower gains while the lender loses.

Student Alert: Inflation is an increase in the price level in the economy. It does not necessarily mean that the price of every good is going up!

Measuring Price Changes

A *price index* is used to measure price changes in the economy. Price indices combine the prices of a bundle of goods and services and track changes in the price of that bundle over time. The Consumer Price Index, or CPI, is the most familiar price index. It measures changes in the price of a bundle of goods and services commonly bought by consumers. The CPI is based on a market basket of more than 200 categories of goods and services weighted according to how much the average consumer spends on them. Two other price indices are the Producer Price Index (PPI) and the GDP deflator. The PPI measures the average change over time in the selling prices received by domestic producers for their output. The GDP price deflator is the most inclusive index because it takes into account the prices of all goods and services produced.

To construct any price index, economists select a year to serve as the base year (the year used for comparison). The prices of other periods are expressed as a percentage of the base period. The value of a price index in the base year is 100, because prices in the base year are 100 percent of prices in that year. Inflation will raise the price of the market basket, and the price index will rise. Deflation will decrease the price of the market basket, and the price index will fall.

For the CPI, the formula used to measure price change from the base period is

$$\text{CPI} = \frac{\text{cost of market basket in current-year prices}}{\text{cost of market basket in base-year prices}} \times 100.$$

Who Is Hurt and Who Is Helped by Unanticipated Inflation?

Identify whether each of the following examples leads to a person or group being hurt or helped by unanticipated inflation. Circle your response, and explain your answer.

H - the person or group is *hurt* by unanticipated inflation
G - the person or group *gains* from unanticipated inflation
U - it is *uncertain* if the person or group is affected by unanticipated inflation

1. Banks extend many fixed-rate loans. →*lenders*

   (H)   G   U

   Explain:

2. A farmer buys machinery with a fixed-rate loan to be repaid over a ten-year period.

   H   (G)   U

   Explain: *paying back money & it won't be worth as much*

3. Your family buys a new home with an adjustable-rate mortgage.

   H   G   (U)

   Explain: *you don't know the interest rate is.*

4. Your savings from your summer job are in a savings account paying a fixed rate of interest.

   (H)   G   U

   Explain: *dont know rate of interest*
   Less money bc inflation may out weigh interest.

5. A widow lives entirely on income from fixed-rate corporate bonds.

   (H)   G   U

   Explain:

6. A retired couple lives entirely on income from a fixed-rate pension the woman receives from her former employer.

H ← *makes more sense*   G   (U)

Explain: *pensions can have a cost of living adjustment*

7. A retired man lines entirely on income from Social Security. ← *can be adjusted*

H ← *good answer.*   G   (U)

Explain:

8. A retired bank official lives entirely on income from stock dividends. → *you own a stock and regardless of what happened to it you get rewarded)*

H   G   (U)

Explain: *dont know what the dividend is.*

9. The federal government has a $14 trillion debt.

H   (G)   U

Explain: *debt must be repayed and when payed off it wont be worth as much.*

10. A firm signs a contract to provide maintenance services at a fixed rate for the next five years.

(H)   G   U

Explain:

11. A state government receives revenue mainly from an income tax.

H   G   (U)

Explain: *depends on how much income tax increase relative to inflation*

12. A local government receives revenue mainly from fixed-rate license fees charged to businesses.

    (H)   G   U

    Explain:

13. Your friend rents an apartment with a three-year lease.

    H   (G)   U

    Explain:

14. A bank has loaned millions of dollars for home mortgages at a fixed rate of interest.

    (H)   G   U

    Explain:

15. Parents are putting savings for their child's college education in a bank savings account.

    H   G   (U)

    Explain:

Price Indices and Real versus Nominal Values

Real versus Nominal Values

Prices in an economy do not stay the same. Over time the price level changes (i.e., there is inflation or deflation). A change in the price level changes the value of economic measures denominated in dollars. Values that increase or decrease with the price level are called *nominal* values. *Real* values are adjusted for price changes. That is, they are calculated as though prices did not change from the base year. For example, gross domestic product (GDP) is used to measure fluctuations in output. However, since GDP is the *dollar value* of goods and services produced in the economy, it increases when prices increase. This means that nominal GDP increases with inflation and decreases with deflation. But when GDP is used as a measure of short-run economic growth, we are interested in measuring increases or decreases in *output*, not prices. That is why real GDP is a better measure of economic performance—real GDP takes out the effects of price changes and allows us to isolate changes in output. Price indices are used to adjust for price changes. They are used to convert nominal values into real values.

Calculating Price Indices

The first step in converting nominal values to real values is to create a price index. A price index compares the total cost of a fixed market basket of goods in different years. The total cost of the market basket is found by multiplying the price of each item in the basket by the quantity of the item in the basket and then summing the results for all items. The cost of the market basket in the current year is then divided by the cost of the basic market basket in the base year as shown below:

$$\text{Price index} = \frac{\text{current-year cost}}{\text{base-year cost}} \times 100.$$

Multiplying by 100 allows comparison of the index in each year to the base-year index value of 100. The base year always has an index number of 100 since the current-year cost and the base-year cost of the market basket are the same in the base year.

The Consumer Price Index (CPI) is a commonly used price index that measures the price of a market basket of consumer goods. The following example shows how the CPI can be used to measure inflation.

Assume an average consumer buys only three items, as shown in Table 2-4.1.

Table 2-4.1
Prices of Three Goods Compared with Base-Year Price

	Quantity bought in base year	Unit price in base year	Spending in base year	Unit price in Year 1	Spending in Year 1	Unit price in Year 2	Spending in Year 2
Whole pizza	30	$5.00	150	$7.00	210	$9.00	270
Flash drive	40	$6.00	240	$5.00	200	$4.00	160
Six-pack of soda	60	$1.50	90	$2.00	120	$2.50	150
Total	–	–	480	–	530	–	580

Fill in the blanks in Table 2-4.1.

1. How much would $100 of goods and services purchased in the base year cost in Year 1?

price index = $\frac{530}{480} \times 100 = \$110$

2. What was the percentage increase in prices in this case? Show your calculations.

$\frac{110}{100} = 10\%$

The rate of change in this index is determined by looking at the percentage change from one year to the next. If, for example, the CPI were 150 in one year and 165 the next, then the year-to-year percentage change is 10 percent. You can compute the change using this formula:

$$\text{Price change} = \frac{\text{change in CPI}}{\text{beginning CPI}} \times 100.$$

3. What is the percentage increase in prices from the base year to Year 2? ___21%___

$\frac{580}{480} \times 100 = 120.8$

121

Table 2-4.2
Constructing a Price Index

Basic market basket item	No. of units	Year 1 Price per unit	Year 1 Cost of market basket	Year 2 Price per unit	Year 2 Cost of market basket	Year 3 Price per unit	Year 3 Cost of market basket
Cheese	2 lbs.	$1.75	$3.50	$1.50	$3.00	$1.50	$3.00
Blue jeans	2 pair	$12.00	$24.00	$15.50	31.00	$20.00	$40.00
Gasoline	10 gals.	$1.25	$12.50	$1.60	$16.00	$2.70	27.00
Total	–	–	$40.00	–	$50.00	–	70.00

Fill in the blanks in Table 2-4.2.

4. If Year 1 is selected as the base year, calculate the price index for each year. Show your work.

(A) Year 1 = ___$100___ $\frac{40}{40} \times 100 =$

(B) Year 2 = ___$125___ $\frac{50}{40} \times 100 = 125$

(C) Year 3 = ___$175___ $\frac{70}{40} \times 100 = 175$

5. These price indices indicate that there was a 25 percent increase in prices between Year 1 and Year 2.

(A) What is the percentage increase between Year 1 and Year 3? ___75%___.

(B) What is the percentage increase between Year 2 and Year 3? ___40%___. $\frac{50}{125} \times 100$

Converting Nominal GDP to Real GDP

To use GDP to measure output growth, it must be converted from nominal to real. Let's say nominal GDP in Year 1 is $1,000 and in Year 2 it is $1,100. Does this mean the economy has grown 10 percent between Year 1 and Year 2? Not necessarily. If prices have risen, part of the increase in nominal GDP in Year 2 will represent the increase in prices. GDP that has been adjusted for price changes is called *real* GDP. If GDP isn't adjusted for price changes, we call it *nominal* GDP.

To compute real GDP in a given year, use the following formula:

Real GDP = nominal GDP/(price index/100).

To compute real output growth in GDP from one year to another, subtract real GDP for Year 2 from real GDP in Year 1. Divide the answer (the change in real GDP from the previous year) by real GDP in Year 1. The result, multiplied by 100, is the percentage growth in real GDP from Year 1 to Year 2. (If real GDP declines from Year 1 to Year 2, the answer will be a negative percentage.) Here's the formula:

$$\text{Output growth} = \frac{(\text{real GDP in Year 2} - \text{real GDP in Year 1})}{\text{real GDP in Year 1}} \times 100.$$

For example, if real GDP in Year 1 = $1,000 and in Year 2 = $1,028, then the output growth rate from Year 1 to Year 2 is 2.8%: (1,028 − 1,000) / 1,000 = .028, which we multiply by 100 in order to express the result as a percentage.

To understand the impact of output changes, we usually look at real GDP per capita. To do so, we divide the real GDP of any period by a country's average population during the same period. This procedure enables us to determine how much of the output growth of a country simply went to supply the increase in population and how much of the growth represented improvements in the standard of living of the entire population. In our example, let's say the population in Year 1 was 100 and in Year 2 it was 110. What was real GDP per capita in Years 1 and 2?

Year 1

$$\text{Real GDP per capita} = \frac{\text{Year 1 real GDP}}{\text{population in Year 1}} = \frac{\$1,000}{100} = \$10.$$

Year 2

$$\text{Real GDP per capita} = \frac{\$1,028}{110} = \$9.30.$$

In this example, real GDP per capita fell even though output growth was positive. Developing countries with positive output growth but high rates of population growth often experience this condition.

Use the information in Table 2-4.3 to answer the following questions.

Table 2-4.3
Nominal and Real GDP

$Real GDP = \dfrac{nominal GDP}{(price index/100)}$

	Nominal GDP	Price index	Population
Year 3	$5,000	125	11
Year 4	$6,000	150	12

6,600

4,000

6. What is the real GDP in Year 3? __$4,000__ $\dfrac{5,000}{\left(\frac{125}{100}\right)}$

4,400

7. What is the real GDP in Year 4? __$4,000__ $\dfrac{6,000}{\left(\frac{150}{100}\right)}$

364

8. What is the real GDP per capita in Year 3? __364__ $\dfrac{4,000}{11} = 363.6$

367

9. What is the real GDP per capita in Year 4? __333__ $\dfrac{4,000}{12} = 333.3$

10%

10. What is the rate of real output growth between Years 3 and 4? __0__

$\dfrac{4,400 - 4,000}{4,000}$

0.8

11. What is the rate of real output growth per capita between Years 3 and 4? __9__
(*Hint:* Use per capita data in the output growth rate formula.)

$\left(\dfrac{364 - 333}{364}\right) \times 100$

8.5

The Costs of Inflation

Unanticipated inflation helps some people and hurts others. For example, borrowers are helped by unanticipated inflation while lenders are hurt. However, even anticipated inflation results in costs for the economy. There are three types of costs that result from inflation: shoe leather costs, menu costs, and unit of account costs.

Shoe leather costs: increased transaction costs caused by inflation.

    The term *shoe leather costs* comes from the idea that inflation results in the need for more trips to the bank and store, wearing out peoples' shoe leather. While technological advances have decreased the amount of walking required to conduct transactions, shoe leather costs still exist in the form of actions that people must take as a result of inflation. Shoe leather costs can be quite substantial in an economy with *hyperinflation* (very high inflation rates).

Menu costs: the cost of changing a listed price.

    Inflation requires firms to incur a cost to change their prices. As a result of inflation, firms must change the tag on the product or shelf, the information attached to a UPC code in a computer, the sticker price on a car, or reprint a restaurant menu (the origin of the term). With hyperinflation, menu costs can cause consumers and merchants to abandon prices listed in their local currency. Menu costs can be substantial in times of high inflation.

Unit of account costs: the cost of having a less reliable unit of measurement.

    One of the uses of money is as a unit of account. Prices are used to compare the value of goods and services. Inflation can decrease the usefulness of prices for comparisons because it changes the purchasing power of a currency over time.

1. For each situation, place an X in the box representing the cost of inflation that is best represented.

Situation	Shoe leather costs	Menu costs	Unit of account costs
(A) Your favorite local restaurant raises its prices and has to print new advertisements.		X	
(B) Workers in Germany in 1922 are paid and shop three times a day due to hyperinflation.	X		
(C) You have to change your automatic bill payment in your online banking account because the rent for your apartment went up.	X		
(D) You remember when the price of gasoline was $1.25 per gallon.			X
(E) You work at your local grocery store and place new higher price stickers on the store's shelves.		X	
(F) Your weekly grocery bill increases, but the amount of groceries you purchase does not.			X

Unemployment

The level of employment is an important measure of economic performance. The unemployment rate measures how well we are achieving the goal of full employment. It is found using a national survey of about 60,000 households. Each month the federal government asks these households about the employment status of household members aged 16 and older (the adult population). The survey puts each person in one of three categories: employed, unemployed, and not in the labor force. People who are at work (the employed) plus those who are not working but are actively looking for work (the unemployed) make up the *labor force*. People who are not working and are not seeking a job are not in the labor force. The category "not in the labor force" includes individuals who are unable to work or choose not to work.

Measuring Unemployment

Only those people who are willing and able to work are considered part of the labor force. The size of the labor force as a percentage of the total population measures the labor resources available to produce in the economy. The *labor force participation rate* (LFPR) is defined as the percentage of the population that is considered part of the labor force.

$$LFPR = \frac{labor\ force}{population} \times 100.$$

The *unemployment rate* (UR) is defined as the number of people who are unemployed as a percentage of the labor force.

$$UR = \frac{number\ of\ unemployed}{labor\ force} \times 100.$$

Student Alert: A person must be actively seeking a job to be considered unemployed. The LFPR is the labor force as a percentage of the *population*. The UR is the number of people unemployed as a percentage of the *labor force*. Make sure to use the right denominator!

1. Fill in the last three columns of Table 2-6.1. All of the population and labor-force data are in millions.

Table 2-6.1
Civilian Employment

Year	Civilian non-institutional population age 16 and over	Civilian labor force			UR	LFPR
		Employed	Unemployed	Total		
1970	117	66	4	70	6%	60%
1980	137	79	4	83	5%	61%
1990	168	99	8	107	7%	64%
2000	188	117	7	125	6%	66%
2010	209	135	6	141	4%	67%

Types of Unemployment

The unemployment rate measures unemployment in the economy but it does not provide information about *why* people are unemployed. To better understand unemployment in the economy, unemployment is classified based on the reason people are willing and able to work but can't find a job. There are three types of unemployment:

■ *Frictional unemployment* includes people who are temporarily between jobs. They may have quit one job to find another, or they could be trying to find the best opportunity after graduating from high school or college.

■ *Cyclical unemployment* includes people who are not working because firms do not need their labor due to a lack of demand or a downturn in the economy. Cyclical unemployment is due to the business cycle.

■ *Structural unemployment* involves mismatches between job seekers and job openings. Unemployed people who lack skills or do not have sufficient education for available jobs are structurally unemployed.

There will always be some frictional and structural unemployment in the economy because people are always moving and changing jobs and because the structure of the economy is always changing, for example, as technology changes. Cyclical unemployment will exist or not, depending on the phase of the business cycle the economy is experiencing.

For each of the following situations, put the appropriate letter before the example.

F if it is an example of *frictional* unemployment.
C if it is an example of *cyclical* unemployment.
S if it is an example of *structural* unemployment.
N if it is an example of someone who is *not* employed.

C 2. A computer programmer is laid off because of a recession.

F 3. A literary editor leaves her job in New York to look for a new job in San Francisco.

F 4. An unemployed college graduate is looking for his first job.

C 5. Advances in technology make the assembly-line worker's job obsolete.

C 6. Slumping sales lead to the cashier being laid off.

N 7. An individual refuses to work for minimum wage.

S 8. A high school graduate lacks the skills necessary for a particular job.

C 9. Workers are laid off when the local manufacturing plant closes because the product made there isn't selling during a recession.

C 10. A skilled glass blower becomes unemployed when a new machine does her job faster.

S 11. An individual has been laid off during a recession and has been looking for work unsuccessfully for so long that he has finally given up actively seeking a job. (*Note:* This person is known as a *discouraged* worker.)

N 12. A college graduate works at a job that does not require a college education.

Circle the letter of each correct answer.

1. In the circular flow diagram, which of the following is true in the product market?

   (A) Households sell goods and services to business firms.

   (B) Households sell resources to business firms.

   (C) Business firms sell resources to households.

   (D) Business firms sell goods and services to households.

   (E) Households buy resources from business firms.

2. In the circular flow diagram, which of the following is true in resource (factor) markets?

   (A) Households buy resources from business firms.

   (B) Households sell products to business firms.

   (C) Households sell resources to business firms.

   (D) Business firms sell goods and services to households.

   (E) Business firms sell resources to households.

3. Which of the following is the best measure of the production (output) of an economy?

   (A) Consumer price index

   (B) Unemployment rate

   (C) Gross domestic product *GDP*

   (D) Prime rate

   (E) Index of leading indicators

4. The market value of all final goods and services produced in the economy in a given year is

   (A) net national product.

   (B) national income.

   (C) personal income.

   (D) gross domestic product. *GDP*

   (E) producer price index.

5. Which of the following people would be considered unemployed?

   (A) A person who quits work to care for aging parents

   (B) A person who stayed home to raise his children and now starts looking for a job

   (C) A person who quits a job to return to school full time

   (D) A person who is qualified to teach but is driving a bus until a teaching job is available

   (E) A person who works two part-time jobs but is looking for a full-time job

6. In the gross domestic product, the largest dollar amount is *expenditure*

   (A) consumer spending. *75%*

   (B) rental payments.

   (C) net exports of goods and services.

   (D) gross private domestic investment.

   (E) government purchases of goods and services.

7. The largest dollar amount of national income is *income*

   (A) rental payments.

   (B) government expenditures on goods and services.

   (C) profit.

   (D) net interest.

   (E) wages and salaries to employees.

8. Which of the following purchases is included in the calculation of gross domestic product?

   (A) A used economics textbook from the bookstore

   (B) New harvesting equipment for the farm

   (C) 1,000 shares of stock in a computer firm

   (D) A car produced in a foreign country

   (E) Government bonds issued by a foreign firm

9. Which of the following would be included in the calculation of gross domestic product?

   (A) Government purchase of a new submarine

   (B) Social Security payment to a retired military officer

   (C) The purchase of a home built 10 years ago

   (D) Contributions to a charity organization

   (E) Work performed by a barber who cuts the hair of his or her own children

10. Which of the following would be counted as investment when calculating gross domestic product?

    (A) The purchase of a used computer by an auto manufacturer   2nd hand sale

    (B) The purchase of a share of IBM stock by an employee

    (C) The construction of a new house

    (D) The construction of roads by the government

    (E) The profit earned when selling shares of stock   shares

11. Which of the following would be an example of an *intermediate* good or service?

    (A) A calculator purchased by a college student for taking exams

    (B) Gasoline purchased by an insurance agent to visit clients at their homes

    (C) A house purchased by a family with four children

    (D) A car purchased by a student's parents and given to the student

    (E) Tuition paid by a student at a state university

12. Of the following, which is the best example of structural unemployment?

    (A) A computer programmer who quits her job to move to a warmer climate

    (B) A construction worker who loses his job in the winter

    (C) An auto worker who loses her job during a recession

    (D) A steel worker who is replaced by a robot

    (E) A toy maker who worked for a company that closed because consumers did not buy its toys

13. If the price index in a country were 100 for the year 2010 and 120 for 2015 and nominal gross domestic product in 2015 were $480 billion, then real gross domestic product for 2015 in 2010 dollars would be

    (A) about $360 billion.

    (B) about $380 billion.

    (C) about $400 billion.

    (D) about $600 billion.

    (E) indeterminate with the given information.

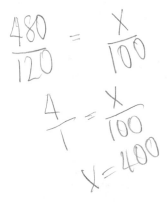

$$\frac{480}{120} = \frac{X}{100}$$

$$\frac{4}{1} = \frac{X}{100}$$

$$X = 400$$

Use the following information for a hypothetical economy to answer questions 14 and 15.

Year	Current or nominal GDP	GDP price deflator index (2000 = 100)	GDP price deflator index (2010 = 100)
2000	$500	100	
2010	$1,200	200	100

14. The value of the gross domestic product in 2010, in terms of 2000 prices, was

(A) $600.

(B) $700.

(C) $1,000.

(D) $1,200.

(E) $1,300.

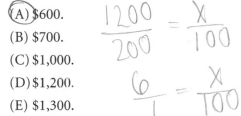

15. If 2010 were made the base year for the GDP price deflator index, the value of the index number for 2000 (rounded to the nearest whole number) would be

(A) 0.

(B) 42.

(C) 142.

(D) 212.

(E) 256.

16. Which of the costs of inflation does the following statement illustrate? "When there is inflation, grocery stores have to update the prices associated with the bar codes on their products."

(A) Menu costs

(B) Shoe leather costs

(C) Unit of account costs

(D) Nominal costs

(E) Time costs

17. Which of the following is a leakage from the circular flow of economic activity?

(A) Saving

(B) Investment

(C) Exports

(D) Government spending

(E) Income

18. Suppose a factory added $5,000 worth of output this year. Incidentally, the waste from this factory caused $1,000 worth of loss to the neighboring waterways. As a result, gross domestic product will

(A) increase by $5,000.

(B) increase by $4,000.

(C) increase by $1,000.

(D) decrease by $4,000.

(E) decrease by $1,000.

19. Which of the following is true if real GDP in Year 1 is $5,000 and in Year 2 is $5,200?

(A) Output has increased by 4 percent.

(B) Output has declined by 4 percent.

(C) Output change is uncertain.

(D) The economy is experiencing 4 percent inflation.

(E) The economy is experiencing a recession.

20. When the actual inflation rate is greater than the anticipated inflation rate, which of the following is most likely to suffer?

(A) Those who lend at a fixed interest rate

(B) Those who borrow at a fixed interest rate

(C) Retired persons with a cost-of-living adjustment in their benefits

(D) Employers who hire workers with long-term labor contracts

(E) Those who lend with flexible interest rates

MACROECONOMICS

National Income and Price Determination

Unit 3

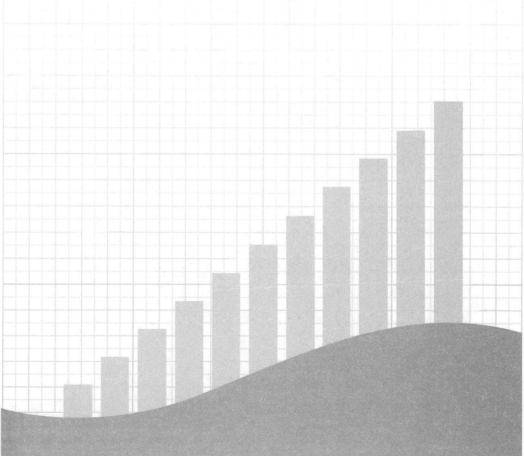

- Aggregate demand (AD) and aggregate supply (AS) curves look and operate much like the market supply and demand curves used in microeconomics. However, *aggregate* demand and *aggregate* supply curves depict somewhat different concepts, and they change for different reasons. AD and AS curves are used to illustrate changes in real output and the price level of an economy.

- The downward slope of the AD curve is explained by the *interest rate effect*, the *wealth effect*, and the *net export effect*. The wealth effect is also called the real-balance effect.

- The upward slope of the short-run aggregate supply curve (SRAS) is explained by fixed input costs (e.g., sticky wages). The long-run aggregate supply (LRAS) curve is vertical at the full-employment level of output.

- The *marginal propensity to consume* (MPC) is the additional consumption spending from an additional dollar of income. The *marginal propensity to save* (MPS) is the additional savings from an additional dollar of income.

$$MPC + MPS = 1.$$

- The spending *multiplier* shows the relationship between changes in spending and the maximum resulting changes in real gross domestic product (GDP). The simple spending multiplier is given as:

$$\text{Spending multiplier} = \frac{1}{1 - MPC} = \frac{1}{MPS}.$$

- Shifts in AD can change the level of output, the price level or both. The determinants of AD include consumer spending, investment spending, government spending, net export spending, and government policies.

- Shifts in SRAS can also change the level of output and the price level. The determinants of SRAS include changes in input prices, productivity, the legal institutional environment, and the quantity of available resources.

- There are two types of inflation: *demand-pull inflation* and *cost-push inflation*. When high unemployment occurs along with high inflation, it is known as stagflation.

- The LRAS curve is vertical at the full-employment level of output.

- In the short run, equilibrium levels of GDP can occur at less than, greater than, or at the full-employment level of GDP. Long-run equilibrium can occur only at full employment.

An Introduction to Aggregate Demand

Why Is the Aggregate Demand Curve Downward Sloping?

Aggregate demand (AD) shows the relationship between real gross domestic product (GDP) and the price level in the economy. As shown in Figure 3-1.1, the AD curve has a negative slope, showing that as the price level increases, real GDP decreases, and as the price level decreases, real GDP increases. The negative relationship between the price level and real GDP is explained by three different things that happen when the price level changes in the economy. When the price level changes, it affects consumers' purchasing power, interest rates paid by consumers and businesses, and the relative prices of domestic goods and services compared to imported goods and services. The effect of a change in the price level on consumers' purchasing power is called the *wealth effect*. The effect of a change in the price level on interest rates (and therefore interest-sensitive spending by consumers on things like houses and cars and investment spending by businesses) is called the *interest rate effect*. The effect of a change in the price level on imports and exports is called the *net export effect*. These three effects explain why the AD curve has a negative slope.

Student Alert: Make sure that when you label an AS/AD graph you use price level and real GDP. Don't use P and Q—those are MICRO labels!

Figure 3-1.1
Aggregate Demand Curve

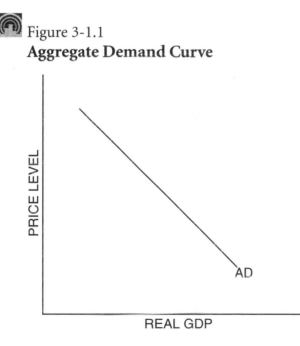

1. Explain how each of the following effects leads to a decrease in real GDP when the price level rises.

   (A) Interest rate effect

   (B) Wealth effect or real balance effect

   (C) Net export effect

What Shifts the Aggregate Demand Curve?

AD is made up of spending by households, businesses, the government, and other countries. The AD curve will shift if there is a change in any of its components: consumption (C), investment (I), government spending (G), or net exports (Xn). As shown in Figure 3-1.2, an increase in AD is shown by a rightward shift of the AD curve, e.g., from AD to AD_1. A decrease in AD is shown by a leftward shift of the AD curve, e.g., from AD to AD_2.

Figure 3-1.2
Shifts in Aggregate Demand

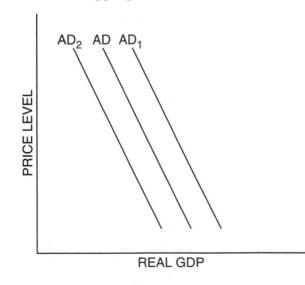

Advanced Placement Economics Macroeconomics: Student Resource Manual © Council for Economic Education, New York, N.Y.

Determine whether each change listed in Table 3-1.1 will cause an increase, decrease, or no change in AD.

2. In column 1, list which component of AD is affected: C, I, G, or Xn.

3. In column 2, draw an up arrow if the change will cause an increase in AD, a down arrow if it will cause a decrease in AD, and write NC if it will not change AD.

4. In column 3, write the number of the AD curve after the change (always start with AD).

 Table 3-1.1

Changes in Aggregate Demand

Change	1. Component of AD	2. Direction of AD change	3. Resulting AD curve
(A) Consumers respond to high levels of debt by reducing their purchases of durable goods.	C	↓	AD 2
(B) Reduced business confidence leads to a reduction in investment spending.	I	↓	AD 2
(C) Government spending increases with no increase in taxes.	G	↑	AD 1
(D) Survey shows consumer confidence jumps.	C	↑	AD 1
(E) Stock market collapses; investors lose billions.	I or C	↓	AD 2
(F) Productivity rises for fourth straight year.	N/A	no change	AD
(G) New tariffs on imported goods lead to a trade war that reduces exports by more than it reduces imports.	Xn	↓	AD 2

no spending = nothing happened

Investment Demand

Investment spending consists of spending on new buildings, machinery, plants, and equipment. Investment spending is a part of aggregate expenditures in the economy. Any increase in investment spending will necessarily increase aggregate expenditures (GDP) and AD.

Decisions about investment spending are based on a comparison of marginal cost and marginal benefit. If a firm expects a particular project to yield a greater benefit than cost, it will undertake it. An important cost associated with investment spending is the interest expense. Firms must either borrow money to engage in an investment project or use their own money. In either case, the interest rate determines the cost of the investment project. If the firm borrows money to invest, it must pay the interest rate to borrow. If the firm uses its own money, then it gives up the interest it could have earned by loaning that money to someone else. That is, the interest rate measures the opportunity cost if a firm invests with its own money.

5. Draw a graph illustrating an investment demand curve. Remember, the price paid to invest is the interest rate, so your graph should show the interest rate on the vertical axis, and the demand curve should have a slope that illustrates the relationship between the interest rate and the amount of investment a firm will undertake.

6. What factors could cause a firm to invest more or less at any given level of the interest rate? That is, what could cause the investment demand curve to shift (increase or decrease)?

The Multiplier

An initial change in any of the components of aggregate demand (AD) will lead to further changes in the economy and an even larger final change in real gross domestic product (GDP). That is, any initial change in spending will be multiplied as it impacts the economy. The final impact of an initial change in spending can be calculated using the *spending multiplier*. The size of the final impact of an initial change in spending on real GDP is affected by the amount of additional spending that results when households receive additional income, called the *marginal propensity to consume*, or MPC. The MPC is the key to understanding the multiplier, so the first step in understanding the multiplier is to understand the MPC.

The MPC is the change in consumption divided by the change in disposable income (DI). It is a fraction of any change in DI that is spent on consumer goods (C): MPC = ΔC / ΔDI.

The *marginal propensity to save (MPS)* is the fraction saved of any change in disposable income. The MPS is equal to the change in saving divided by the change in DI: MPS = ΔS / ΔDI.

The MPC measures *changes* in consumption when income changes. The MPC is distinct from the *average propensity to consume (APC)*, which measures the average amount of the total income households spend or save.

The APC is the ratio of C to disposable income, or APC = C / DI.

The *average propensity to save (APS)* is the ratio of savings (S) to disposable income, or APS = S / DI.

1. Fill in the blanks in Table 3-2.1.

Table 3-2.1
Average Propensities to Consume and to Save C/DI S/DI

Disposable income	Consumption	Saving	APC	APS
$0	$2,000	−$2,000	—	—
$2,000	$3,600	−$1,600	1.8	−0.8
$4,000	$5,200	−$1,200	1.2	−0.2
$6,000	$6,800	$800	1.1	−0.1
$8,000	$8,400	−$400	1.05	−0.05
$10,000	$10,000	$0	1	0
$12,000	$11,600	$400	0.96	0.03

2.   Fill in the blanks in Table 3-2.2.

Table 3-2.2
Marginal Propensities to Consume and to Save   C/DI   S/DI

Disposable income	Consumption	Saving	MPC	MPS
$12,000	$12,100	–$100	—	—
$13,000	$13,000	$0	0.90	0.10
$14,000	$13,800	$200	0.99	0.01
$15,000	$14,500	$500	0.97	0.03
$16,000	$15,100	$900	0.94	0.06
$17,000	$18,800	$1,400	1.105	0.08

3.   Explain why the sum of MPC and MPS must always equal 1.

You can only consume or save as much money as you income.

The Multiplier

The following example illustrates how an initial change in a component of AD results in an even larger change in real GDP (i.e., the multiplier process).

The people in Econoland live on an isolated island. One year a stranger arrives and builds a factory to make seashell charms. The factory is considered an investment on Econoland. If the MPC on the island is 75 percent, or 0.75, it means that Econoland residents consume 75 percent of any change in income and save 25 percent of any change in income. The additional spending generates additional income and eventually a multiple increase in income. This is called the *multiplier effect*. When they hear about the multiplier effect, the islanders are thrilled about the new factory because they like the idea of additional income.

The residents of Econoland want to know what would eventually happen to the levels of GDP, consumption, and saving on the island as the new spending works its way through the economy. Luckily there is a retired economist on Econoland who offers a brief statement of the multiplier. "It's simple," he says, "One person's spending becomes another person's income." The economist gives a numerical example, as shown in Table 3-2.3. "This shows the process," he says. The rounds refer to the movement of spending from resident to resident. His example stops at four rounds and the rest of the rounds are added together to cover the total effect on all Econoland's citizens.

 Table 3-2.3

Changes in Econoland's GDP, Consumption, and Saving

Round	Income (GDP)	Consumption spending	Saving
Round 1	$1,000	0.75 of $1,000 = $750.00	0.25 of $1,000 = $250.00
Round 2	One person's spending becoming another person's income: $750.00	0.75 of $750 = $562.50	0.25 of $750 = $187.50
Round 3	The next person's spending becoming another person's income: $562.50	0.75 of $562.50 = $421.88	0.25 of $562.50 = $140.62
Round 4	The next person's spending becoming another person's income: $421.88	0.75 of $421.88 = $316.41	0.25 of $421.88 = $105.47
Rounds continue	. . .	. . .	. . .
All rounds	Final outcome for income (GDP) 1 / (1 − 0.75) x $1,000 = 4 x $1,000 = $4,000	Final outcome for consumption spending 0.75 of $4,000 = $3,000	Final outcome for saving 0.25 of $4,000 = $1,000

The retired economist summarizes the multiplier effect for the crowd of Econolanders. "This shows us that the factory is an investment that has a multiplied effect on our GDP. In this case, the multiplier is 4." He adds, "It appears to be magic, but it is simply that *one person's spending becomes another person's income.*" The islanders nod with agreement but also look puzzled, so the old professor asks the citizens a series of questions. How would Econlanders answer these questions?

4. Would the multiplier be larger or smaller if you saved more of your additional income?

The multiplier would be less if you saved more

5. What do you think would happen if all Econolanders saved all of the change in their incomes?

Nothing would be spent therefore unemployment would decrease as well as other things

6. What would happen if you spent *all* of the change in your income?

The professor then points out that a new road around the island or a new bridge built by the island government over the lagoon would also have a multiplied effect on GDP. He also tells them that if the government of Econoland lowers taxes, the citizens would have more income to spend, which would cause a multiplier effect. He notes that there is another side to this. If taxes are raised, there is a multiplier effect, which decreases income and GDP by a multiple amount.

Multiplier Formulas and Terms

MPC = ΔC / ΔDI

MPS = ΔS / ΔDI

Spending Multiplier = 1 / (1 – MPC) or 1 / MPS

How to use the spending multiplier:

Change in GDP = change in AD component x spending multiplier.

When to use the spending multiplier:

When there is a change in a component of AD.

When the government changes taxes, it will also affect AD. If taxes are decreased, consumers (or businesses) have more disposable income and will increase spending. When the government raises taxes, households (or businesses) have less disposable income and will decrease spending. The basic multiplier effect is the same, but with two differences. First, increasing taxes decreases spending, and decreasing taxes increases spending. The effect of taxes on spending is negative, so the tax multiplier has a negative sign. Second, taxes are not a component of AD. When taxes change, consumers (or businesses) will change their spending by only part of that amount, determined by the MPC. So, for every additional dollar in disposable income, spending will only increase by $MPC. Therefore, the numerator of the tax multiplier is MPC, rather than 1.

🛈 *Student Alert:* **Make sure to use the tax multiplier when the change affecting AD is a change in taxes!**

Tax Multiplier = –MPC /(1 – MPC) = – MPC /MPS

How to use the tax multiplier:

Change in GDP = change in taxes x tax multiplier.

When to use the tax multiplier:

When there is a change in lump-sum taxes.

Note: Remember that the tax multiplier has a negative sign.

Quick Quiz on Multipliers

7. What is the value of the tax multiplier if the MPC is 0.80? ___-4___

$$\frac{-0.80}{0.20}$$

8. What is the value of the spending multiplier if the MPC is 0.67? ___3___

$$1 - 0.67 = 0.33 \qquad \frac{1}{0.33} \circ \left(\frac{1}{1-0.67}\right)$$

9. What is the tax multiplier if the MPS is 0.25? ___-3___

MPC is 0.75 $\dfrac{-0.75}{0.25}$

Advanced Placement Economics Macroeconomics: Student Resource Manual © Council for Economic Education, New York, N.Y.

An Introduction to Short-Run Aggregate Supply

Why Is the Short-Run Aggregate Supply Curve Upward Sloping?

The short-run aggregate supply (SRAS) curve shows the relationship between real gross domestic product (GDP) and the price level. This positive relationship exists because producers seek to maximize profits and production costs are inflexible. Since firms seek to maximize profits, change in the price level will affect the quantity that they produce. When the price level rises, but production costs stay the same, firms make more profit on each unit sold, so they increase the quantity that they produce. When the price level decreases, but production costs stay the same, firms make less profit, and they reduce the quantity that they produce. In the long run, when production costs are flexible, this relationship does not hold true. But in the short run, inflexible production costs lead to a positive relationship between the price level and real GDP and therefore an upward sloping SRAS curve.

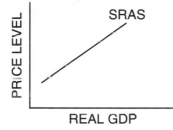

What Shifts the Short-Run Aggregate Supply Curve?

SRAS will increase if firms produce more at any given price level, and it will decrease if firms produce less at any given price level. Therefore, the SRAS curve will shift as a result of changes in input prices (e.g., nominal wages or oil prices) or productivity (e.g., technological advances), as shown in Figure 3-3.1.

Figure 3-3.1
Shifts in Short-Run Aggregate Supply

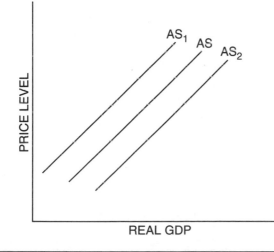

1. Determine whether each change listed in Table 3-3.1 will cause an increase, decrease, or no change in aggregate supply (AS). Always start with AS.

2. In column 1, list which component of AS is affected: input prices or productivity.

3. In column 2, draw an up arrow if the change will cause an increase in AS, a down arrow if it will cause a decrease in AS, and write NC if it will not change AS.

4. In column 3, write the number of the AS curve after the change.

Table 3-3.1
Changes in Aggregate Supply

Change	1. Determinant of AS	2. Change in AS	3. Resulting AS curve
(A) Unions are more effective so that wage rates increase.			
(B) OPEC successfully increases oil prices.			
(C) Labor productivity increases dramatically.			
(D) Giant natural gas discovery decreases energy prices.			
(E) Computer technology brings new efficiency to industry.			
(F) Government spending increases.			
(G) Cuts in tax rates increase incentives to save and invest.			
(H) Low birth rate will decrease the labor force in the future.			
(I) Research shows that improved schools have increased the skills of American workers and managers.			

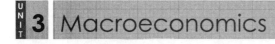
Possible Shapes of Short-Run Aggregate Supply Curve

In general, the SRAS has a positive slope. However, in special situations, the SRAS may be very flat or very steep, as shown below.

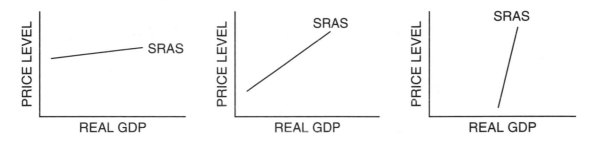

5. What does it tell you about the relationship between the price level and real GDP if the SRAS is flat? Under what conditions would an economy have a flat SRAS curve?

6. What does it tell you about the relationship between the price level and real GDP if the SRAS is steep? Under what conditions would an economy have a steep SRAS curve?

Sticky versus Flexible Wages and Prices

In macroeconomics there is both a short run and a long run. The short run is the time period in which at least one factor is fixed. For example, the price of inputs (hourly wages paid to labor and other unit resource prices) remains fixed, or sticky, in the short run. However, the price of firms' output in the product markets varies directly with the price level. Input prices remain fixed for many reasons, e.g., wage contracts, menu pricing, and delays in recognizing unanticipated inflation. The lag between changes in output prices and changes in input prices results in firms earning short-run profits when there is inflation or losses when there is deflation. The long run in macroeconomics is the period of time in which input prices adjust to changes in the overall price level.

With price level increases, product market prices increase while factor market prices remain fixed. Fixed input prices and higher output prices leads to profit. This profit provides firms with an incentive to increase production. Refer to Figure 3-4.1. Notice that as price level increases from PL$_1$ to PL$_2$ that real gross domestic product (GDP) increases from Y$_1$ to Y$_2$.

The opposite would occur if product market prices fall with a decrease in the price level. Firms experience losses when input prices remain high and output prices decrease. The losses result in a decrease in production which leads to a decrease in real GDP.

The result of firms varying their production directly with changes in the price level is an upward sloping AS curve in the short run. Hence, in the short run, the level of real GDP is directly related to the price level. Figure 3-4.2 illustrates the SRAS.

Figure 3-4.1
Price Level and Real GDP

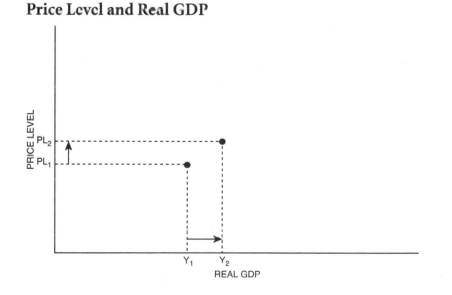

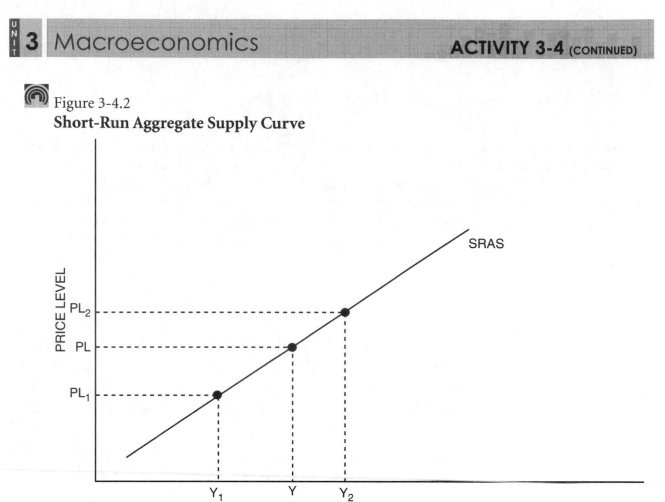

Figure 3-4.2
Short-Run Aggregate Supply Curve

1. Identify at least two reasons that input prices remain fixed in the short run.

2. Explain why firms' profits increase when the price level increases in the short run.

3. Would firms have an incentive to change their level of production if input prices adjusted immediately to output price changes? Why?

4. Review your answers to (2) and (3). Assume that input prices are not fixed, but that they change directly with output prices. If firms are initially producing output Y_1 as seen in the graph below, then an increase in the price level from PL_1 to PL_2 will have what effect on real GDP? Illustrate the relationship between price level and real GDP in the long run, and label it LRAS for long-run aggregate supply.

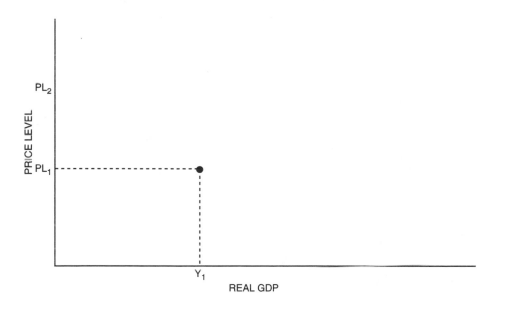

Short-Run Equilibrium Price Level and Output

The first section of the course presented the supply and demand model as a way to determine price and quantity in individual markets. The aggregate supply (AS) and aggregate demand (AD) model uses AS and AD to determine the equilibrium price level and aggregate quantity of output (real GDP) in the economy. It is important to correctly label the AS/AD graph to distinguish it from the market supply and demand graph. As shown in Figure 3-5.1, the axes labels should clearly indicate price level (PL), real GDP (Y), AS, and AD. Equilibrium in the model is found at the intersection of AS and AD. The equilibrium PL is identified on the vertical axis and the equilibrium Y is found on the horizontal axis.

🛈 *Student Alert:* **Make sure you label the equilibrium values on the axes rather than as a point in the middle of the graph.**

Figure 3-5.1
Equilibrium Price and Output Levels

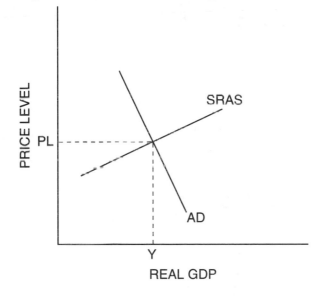

Summarizing Aggregate Demand and Aggregate Supply Shifts

For each of the graphs below, identify the starting equilibrium PL and Y. Then show the shift given for each graph and identify the new equilibrium PL and Y. Indicate the resulting change in price level, unemployment, and real GDP by circling the up arrow for an increase or the down arrow for a decrease.

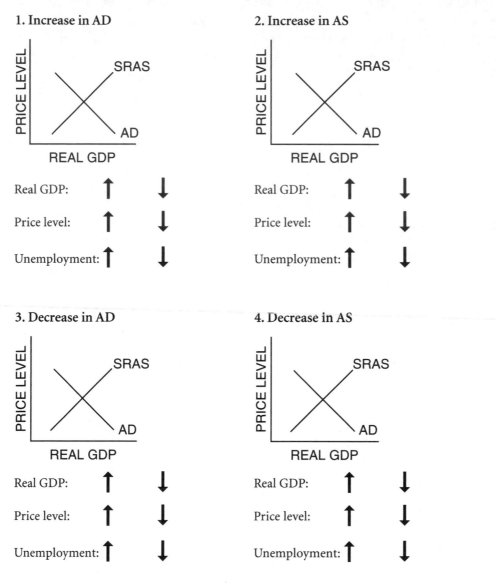

1. Increase in AD

Real GDP: ↑ ↓

Price level: ↑ ↓

Unemployment: ↑ ↓

2. Increase in AS

Real GDP: ↑ ↓

Price level: ↑ ↓

Unemployment: ↑ ↓

3. Decrease in AD

Real GDP: ↑ ↓

Price level: ↑ ↓

Unemployment: ↑ ↓

4. Decrease in AS

Real GDP: ↑ ↓

Price level: ↑ ↓

Unemployment: ↑ ↓

Changes in Short-Run Aggregate Supply and Aggregate Demand

The equilibrium price and quantity in the economy will change when either the short-run aggregate supply (SRAS) or the aggregate demand (AD) curve shifts. The AD curve shifts when any of the components of AD change—consumption (C), investment (I), government spending (G), exports (X), or imports (M). The aggregate supply (AS) curve shifts when there are changes in the price of inputs (e.g., nominal wages, oil prices) or changes in productivity.

Changes in the Equilibrium Price Level and Output

For each situation described below, illustrate the change on the AD and AS graph and describe the effect on the equilibrium price level and real gross domestic product (GDP) by circling the correct symbol: ↑ for increase, ↓ for decrease, or — for unchanged

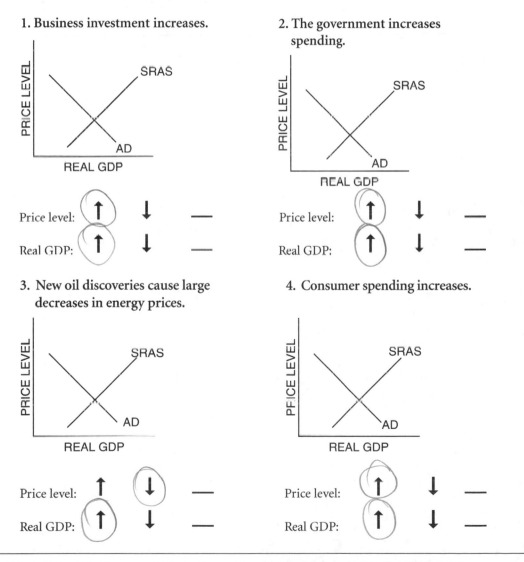

1. Business investment increases.

Price level: (↑) ↓ —

Real GDP: (↑) ↓ —

2. The government increases spending.

Price level: (↑) ↓ —

Real GDP: (↑) ↓ —

3. New oil discoveries cause large decreases in energy prices.

Price level: ↑ (↓) —

Real GDP: (↑) ↓ —

4. Consumer spending increases.

Price level: (↑) ↓ —

Real GDP: (↑) ↓ —

5. Production costs increase.

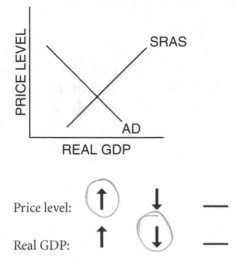

Price level: ⬆(circled) ⬇(circled) —

Real GDP: ⬆ ⬇(circled) —

6. New technology and better education increase labor productivity.

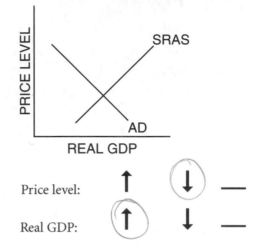

Price level: ⬆ ⬇(circled) —

Real GDP: ⬆(circled) ⬇ —

7. Consumers' confidence improves.

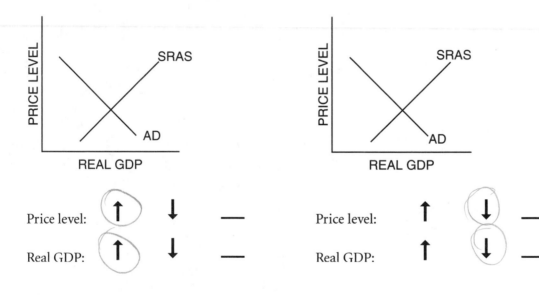

Price level: ⬆(circled) ⬇ —

Real GDP: ⬆(circled) ⬇ —

8. Net exports decrease.

Price level: ⬆ ⬇(circled) —

Real GDP: ⬆ ⬇(circled) —

Graphing Demand and Supply Shocks

Draw an AS/AD graph to illustrate the change given in each of the questions below. On your graph be sure to label the axes (PL and Y), the AS and AD curves, and the starting and ending equilibrium PL and Y (these should be placed on the axes).

9. Economic booms in both Japan and Europe result in massive increases in orders for exported goods from the United States.

AD↑

10. The government reduces taxes and increases transfer payments.

AD↑

11. Fine weather results in the highest corn and wheat yields in 40 years.

AS↑

12. While the United States was in the midst of the Great Depression, a foreign power attacked, Congress declared war, and more than 1,000,000 soldiers were drafted in the first year while defense spending was increased several times over.

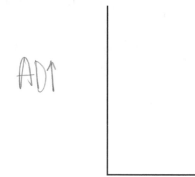

AD↑

13. To balance the budget, the federal government cuts Social Security payments by 10 percent and federal aid to education by 20 percent.

AD↓

14. During a long, slow recovery from a recession, consumers postponed major purchases. Suddenly they begin to buy cars, refrigerators, televisions, and furnaces to replace their failing models.

AD↑

15. In response to other dramatic changes, the government raises taxes and reduces transfer payments in the hope of balancing the federal budget.

AD↓

16. News of possible future layoffs frightens the public into reducing spending and increasing saving for the feared "rainy day."

AD↓

The Types of Inflation

The aggregate supply (AS) and aggregate demand (AD) model is used to determine changes in the price level and real gross domestic product (GDP). Changes in AS and AD lead to changes in the price level (inflation and deflation). Whether changes in the price level are due to changes in AS or AD determines the type of inflation experienced in the economy. Demand-pull inflation is caused by a shift in the AD curve. Cost-push inflation is caused by a shift in the AS curve.

Demand-pull inflation occurs because the demand for goods and services increases at a time when the production of goods and services is already high. The increase in AD causes real GDP to expand and the price level to increase. Demand-pull inflation is often described by the saying "too much money chasing too few goods."

Figure 3-7.1 illustrates demand-pull inflation. An increase in AD causes the AD curve to shift to the right. AD will increase as a result of a change in the determinants of AD: consumption (C), investment (I), government spending (G), and net exports (Xn). Notice that, in addition to the increase in the price level, the increase in AD leads to an increase in real GDP.

Figure 3-7.1

Changes in the Price Level Due to Aggregate Demand

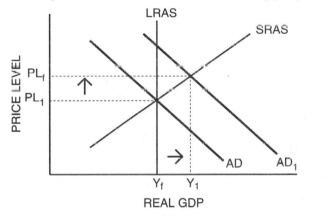

Cost-push inflation is caused by an increase in the cost of an input with economy-wide importance. An increase in production costs throughout the economy will cause AS to decrease. For example, an increase in wages or the price of oil will increase input costs economy-wide.

Figure 3-7.2 illustrates cost-push inflation. A decrease in AS causes the AS curve to shift to the left. AS will decrease as a result of an increase in production costs throughout the economy. Notice that, in addition to the increase in the price level, the decrease in AS leads to a decrease in real GDP. *Stagflation* occurs when the economy experiences high inflation and high unemployment at the same time.

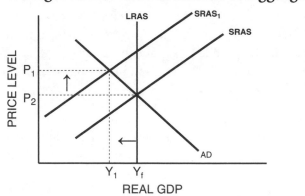

Figure 3-7.2

Changes in the Price Level Due to Aggregate Supply

For each situation described below, circle either demand-pull or cost-push inflation and explain.

1. In his 2020 State of the Union address, President Dodge calls for an increase in the U.S. military presence across the globe to combat what he deemed a "threat to the sovereignty of the U.S. economy and trade routes."

   Demand-Pull Inflation   *Cost-Push Inflation*

   Explain:

2. The Arab Spring of 2010 disrupts oil production and supplies worldwide. This causes OPEC and commodities speculators to raise crude oil prices to record levels.

   Demand-Pull Inflation   *Cost-Push Inflation*

   Explain:

3. During the election of 2100, Democratic presidential candidates all advocate the expansion of the Social Security and Medicare and Medicaid programs to include a greater number of American citizens. These campaign promises cause the United States to run a budget deficit in the year after the election, which in turn leads to increased government borrowing.

Demand-Pull Inflation   *Cost-Push Inflation*

Explain:

4. The federal government raises the minimum wage to $12 an hour.

Demand-Pull Inflation   *Cost-Push Inflation*

Explain:

Long-Run Aggregate Supply

In this activity we move from the short run to the long run. In the short run, at least one factor of production is fixed. In the long run, all factors of production are variable. The short-run aggregate supply (SRAS) curve is upward sloping because of slow wage and price adjustments in the economy. But in the long run, wages and prices have time to adjust. That is, wages and prices are fully flexible. This means that any time the price level changes (i.e., there is inflation or deflation), wages and other input costs fully adjust so there is no overall effect. For example, if prices were doubled and wages and other input costs doubled, there would be no effect. Or if prices were cut in half, but so were wages and other input costs, there would be no effect. In the long run, wages and other input costs adjust so the economy always returns to the full-employment level of output. This means that the long-run aggregate supply (LRAS) curve is vertical at the full-employment output level (which is also called potential output).

Using Figure 3-8.1, answer the following questions about how the economy will react over time if the aggregate demand (AD) shifts from AD to AD_1.

Figure 3-8.1
Increase in Aggregate Demand Starting at Full Employment

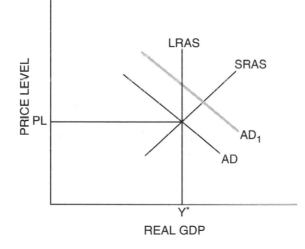

1. What will happen to output, nominal wages and real wages, and the price level in the short run? Explain.

2. What will happen to output and the price level when the economy moves to long-run equilibrium? Explain.

3. On Figure 3-8.1, draw the long-run equilibrium situation (including PL, Y, and AD).

4. Using Figure 3-8.2, answer the following questions about how the economy will react over time if the aggregate supply (AS) shifts from SRAS to SRAS$_1$. Assume that no monetary or fiscal policy is undertaken.

Figure 3-8.2
Change in Short-Run Aggregate Supply

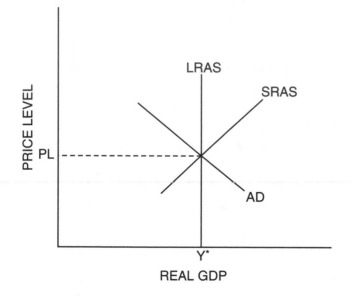

5. After SRAS decreases, what happens to the short-run output, nominal wages, real wages, and the price level?

6. What will happen to output and the price level when the economy moves to long-run equilibrium? Explain.

7. On Figure 3-8.2, draw the long-run equilibrium situation (including PL, Y, and AS).

Read the description of each change in AS or AD. Draw your own graph showing the starting point as long-run equilibrium, illustrated in the graph below. Draw a new SRAS or AD curve that represents the change caused by the event described. Explain the reasons for the short-run change in the graph, and then explain what happens in the long run. Identify the final AD curve as AD_f and the final SRAS curve as $SRAS_f$.

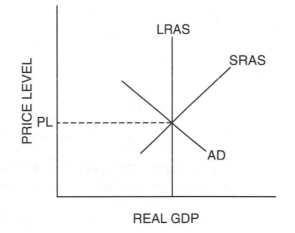

8. The government increases defense spending by 10 percent a year over a five-year period.

9. OPEC cuts oil production by 30 percent, and the world price of oil rises by 40 percent.

10. The government increases spending on education, health care, housing, and basic services for low-income people. No increase in taxes accompanies these programs.

11. Can the government maintain output above the natural level of output with AD policy? If the government attempts to, what will be the result?

Actual versus Full-Employment Output

The model of aggregate demand (AD) and aggregate supply (AS) predicts that the macroeconomy will come to equilibrium at the intersection of a downward-sloping AD curve and an upward-sloping short-run aggregate supply (SRAS) curve. The short-run equilibrium is described as the only price level where the goods and services purchased by domestic and foreign buyers are equal to the quantity supplied within the economy. It's important to realize that, while the economy might be in equilibrium, this equilibrium level of output can be less than, equal to, or greater than full-employment output.

Full-employment output is the level of real gross domestic product (GDP) that exists when the economy's unemployment rate is at its natural rate. This natural rate of unemployment doesn't correspond to an unemployment rate of zero; rather, it is the unemployment rate that exists when there is no cyclical unemployment. When the economy is recessionary, the unemployment rate will exceed this natural rate. When the economy is experiencing an inflationary gap, the unemployment rate will fall below the natural rate.

The distinction between the actual unemployment rate and the natural rate allows us to reconsider the short-run equilibrium in the macroeconomy. If AD and SRAS intersect at a level of output that falls below full-employment output (at the vertical long-run aggregate supply [LRAS] curve), the economy has a recessionary gap. If the AD and SRAS curves intersect at a real output that exceeds full employment, the economy has an inflationary gap.

1. Draw an LRAS curve that illustrates a recessionary gap. Label the full-employment level of output on the graph.

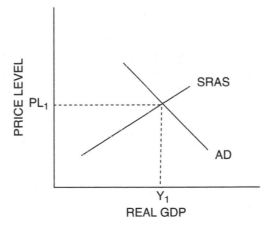

2. Draw an LRAS curve that illustrates an inflationary gap. Label the full-employment level of output on the graph.

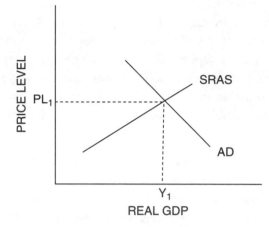

3. Suppose households in the United States experience a decrease in wealth. Assume the economy starts at long-run equilibrium as shown in Figure 3-9.1. Use the AS/AD model to show the short-run effect on output, unemployment, and the price level.

 Figure 3-9.1
Price Level

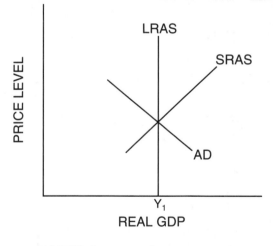

(A) Will the unemployment rate increase or decrease? Explain.

(B) What type of gap results from the decrease in wealth?

Circle the letter of each correct answer.

1. Which of the following best describes the short-run aggregate supply curve?

   (A) The amount buyers plan to spend on output

   (B) A curve showing the relationship between inputs and outputs

   (C) A curve showing the trade-off between inflation and unemployment

   (D) A curve indicating the level of real output that will be purchased at each possible price level

   (E) A curve indicating the level of real output that will be produced at each possible price level

2. A change in which of the following will cause the aggregate demand curve to shift?

   (A) Energy prices

   (B) Productivity rates

   (C) Consumer wealth

   (D) Prices of inputs

   (E) Prices of consumer goods

3. The short-run aggregate supply curve will shift to the right when

   (A) energy prices increase.

   (B) government regulation increases.

   (C) prices of inputs decrease.

   (D) investment spending decreases.

   (E) productivity rates decrease.

4. A rightward shift in the aggregate demand curve will cause employment and the price level to change in which of the following ways in the short run?

	Employment	Price level
(A)	Increase	Increase
(B)	Increase	Decrease
(C)	Increase	No change
(D)	Decrease	Increase
(E)	No change	No change

5. An increase in the capital stock will cause the

   (A) aggregate demand curve to shift left.

   (B) aggregate demand to shift right.

   (C) production possibilities curve to shift in.

   (D) aggregate supply curve to shift left.

   (E) long-run aggregate supply curve to shift right.

6. Which of the following will increase aggregate demand?

   (A) A decrease in personal income taxes

   (B) A decrease in government spending

   (C) An increase in corporate income taxes

   (D) A decrease in the capital stock

   (E) An increase in interest rate

7. An increase in labor productivity would most likely cause real gross domestic product and the price level to change in which of the following ways?

	Real GDP	Price level
(A)	Increase	Increase
(B)	Increase	Decrease
(C)	Increase	No change
(D)	Decrease	Increase
(E)	Decrease	No change

8. If Maria Escalera's disposable income increases from $600 to $650 and her level of personal-consumption expenditures increases from $480 to $520, you may conclude that her marginal propensity to

   (A) consume is 0.8.

   (B) consume is 0.4.

   (C) consume is 0.25.

   (D) save is 0.8.

   (E) save is 0.25.

9. Which effect describes the fact that when the price level increases, the interest rate increases and consumption decreases?

   (A) Interest rate effect

   (B) Net export effect

   (C) Pareto effect

   (D) Substitution effect

   (E) Real balance effect

10. The change in real GDP that occurs when an increase in the price level leads to a change in the relative prices of imports and exports is a result of the

   (A) interest rate effect.

   (B) net export effect.

   (C) Pareto effect.

   (D) substitution effect.

   (E) real balance effect.

11. The short-run aggregate supply curve slopes upward because of

   (A) the wealth effect.

   (B) sticky wages and prices.

   (C) the law of diminishing returns.

   (D) the natural rate of unemployment.

   (E) the multiplier.

12. Investment demand increases as the result of

   (A) excess productive capacity.

   (B) an increase in corporate business taxes.

   (C) businesses becoming more optimistic with respect to future business conditions.

   (D) recessions in foreign nations that trade with the United States, causing a lower demand for U.S. products.

   (E) a decrease in the real interest rate.

13. Which of the following shifts the short-run aggregate supply curve to the right?

   (A) A technological advance

   (B) Rising input prices

   (C) Higher wages

   (D) An increase in government spending

   (E) An increase in oil prices

14. In which of the following ways will increases in short-run aggregate supply change the price level and unemployment?

	Price level	Unemployment
(A)	Increase	No change
(B)	Decrease	Decrease
(C)	Decrease	Increase
(D)	Decrease	No change
(E)	No change	Increase

15. As the average price level decreases, the purchasing power of people's cash balances increases. This results in an increase in spending. This effect is called

   (A) the Laffer effect.

   (B) the Keynesian effect.

   (C) the money illusion effect.

   (D) the real balance effect.

   (E) the neutrality of money.

16. A sustained increase in oil prices would most likely cause short-run and long-run aggregate supply curves and the production possibilities curve to change in which of the following ways?

	SRAS curve	LRAS curve	Production possibilities curve
(A)	Decrease	No change	Shift outward
(B)	Decrease	Decrease	Shift outward
(C)	Decrease	Decrease	Shift inward
(D)	Increase	No change	No change
(E)	Increase	Increase	Shift inward

17. A rapid increase in successful research and development projects for the nation will most likely result in which of the following changes in the short-run and the long-run aggregate supply curves and the production possibilities curve?

	SRAS curve	LRAS curve	Production possibilities curve
(A)	Decrease	No change	No change
(B)	Decrease	Decrease	Shift inward
(C)	Increase	No change	Shift inward
(D)	Increase	Increase	No change
(E)	Increase	Increase	Shift outward

18. The numerical value for the spending multiplier increases as the value of the

(A) MPS decreases.

(B) APC increases.

(C) MPC decreases.

(D) MPS increases.

(E) APC decreases.

19. If the spending multiplier is 5, the value of the tax multiplier must be

(A) 5.   (D) –4.

(B) 4.   (E) –5.

(C) 1.

20. If the marginal propensity to consume is two-thirds, then an increase in personal income taxes of $100 will most likely result in

(A) a decrease in consumption of $100.

(B) a decrease in autonomous investment of $100.

(C) a decrease in consumption of $67 and an increase in savings of $33.

(D) a decrease in consumption of $67 and a decrease in savings of $33.

(E) an increase in government spending of more than $100.

21. An increase in personal income taxes will most likely result in which of the following changes in real GDP and the price level in the short run?

	Real GDP	Price level
(A)	Decrease	Decrease
(B)	Decrease	Increase
(C)	Increase	No change
(D)	Increase	Increase
(E)	Increase	No change

22. One of the reasons the aggregate demand curve is downward sloping is that as the value of cash balances decreases, aggregate spending decreases. This is called

(A) the interest rate effect.

(B) the net export effect.

(C) the Pareto effect.

(D) the substitution effect.

(E) the real balance effect.

23. Rising input price will shift which curve and create which type of inflation?

Curve	Type of inflation
(A) AS	Cost-push
(B) AS	Supply-pull
(C) AD	Cost-push
(D) AD	Demand-pull
(E) AD	Supply-pull

24. "Too much money chasing too few goods" describes which of the following?

    (A) The income effect

    (B) The wealth effect

    (C) Demand-pull inflation

    (D) The real balance effect

    (E) Cost-push inflation

25. Which of the following statements is true about actual employment?

    (A) It must equal full employment.

    (B) It cannot exceed full employment.

    (C) It exceeds full employment in a recession.

    (D) It is below full employment in a recession.

    (E) It is the same as full employment.

MACROECONOMICS

Financial Sector

Unit 4

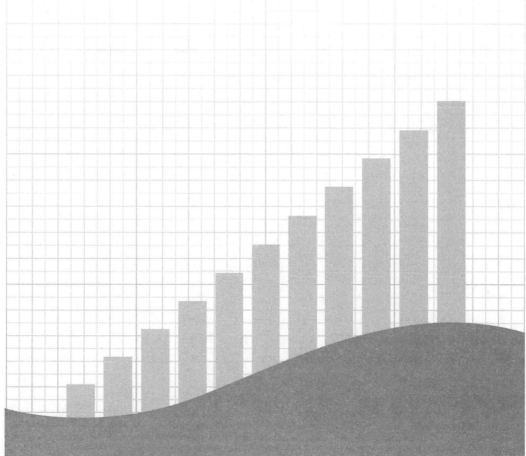

■ Money can take many forms and is defined as anything that serves the three main functions of money: a medium of exchange, a standard of value (or unit of account), and a store of value.

■ Financial assets include stocks and bonds. They represent a claim that entitles the buyer to future income from the seller.

■ Decisions often have consequences that last well into the future. The concept of present value is used to address the issue of timing when measuring costs and benefits.

■ The money supply is measured by *monetary aggregates* including M0, M1, and M2. Each monetary aggregate defines money somewhat differently. The M2, M1, and M0 money supply includes increasingly liquid assets.

■ In a fractional reserve banking system, demand deposits lead to money creation. Money is created through the money multiplier process when banks make loans, and it is destroyed when loans are repaid.

■ Banks are required to keep a percentage of their deposits as reserves. Reserves can be currency in the bank vault or deposits at the Federal Reserve Banks. The reserve requirement limits the amount of money banks can create.

■ The simple deposit expansion multiplier is equal to 1 divided by the required reserve ratio (rr).

Deposit expansion multiplier = 1 / rr

■ The demand for money is the sum of transactions demand, precautionary demand, and speculative demand. The demand for money is determined by interest rates, income, and the price level. The supply of money is set by the Federal Reserve (the Fed). Equilibrium in the money market determines the interest rate in the economy.

■ The loanable funds market is made up of lenders, who supply funds, and borrowers, who demand funds. Equilibrium in the loanable funds market determines the interest rate and quantity of loanable funds.

■ The Federal Reserve regulates financial institutions and controls the nation's money supply. The three main tools that the Fed can use to control the money supply are buying and selling government bonds (open market operations), changing the discount rate, and changing the reserve requirement.

■ If the Fed wants to increase the money supply, it will encourage bank lending by buying bonds, decreasing the discount rate, or decreasing the reserve requirement. This is referred to as expansionary monetary policy and is used by the Fed to reduce unemployment.

■ If the Fed wants to decrease the money supply, it will discourage bank lending by selling bonds, increasing the discount rate, or increasing the reserve requirement. This is called a contractionary monetary policy and is used by the Fed to control inflation.

■ Open market operations are the most frequently used tool. Since changes in the reserve requirement can have substantial economic effects, the Fed rarely changes it.

■ The federal funds rate (ffr) is the interest rate a bank charges when it lends excess reserves to other banks. The Fed currently targets the ffr to implement monetary policy because it is closely tied to economic activity.

■ MV = PQ is the equation of exchange: Money times velocity equals price times quantity of goods. PQ is the nominal GDP. Velocity is the number of times a year that the money supply is used to make payments for final goods and services.

Money and Financial Assets

Money is generally accepted in payment for goods and services and serves as an asset to its holder. Money is anything that serves three important functions: a medium of exchange, a standard of value, and a store of value.

To be a good *medium of exchange*, money must be accepted by people when they buy and sell goods and services. It should be portable or easily carried from place to place. It must also be divisible so that large and small transactions can be made. It must also be uniform so that a particular unit such as a quarter represents the same value as every other quarter.

To be a good *standard of value*, or *unit of account*, money must be useful for denominating values (prices). To accomplish this, money must be familiar, divisible, and accepted.

To be a good *store of value*, money must be durable so it can be kept for future use. It also should have a stable value so people do not lose purchasing power if they use the money at a later time.

Throughout history, a wide variety of items have served as money. These include gold, silver, tobacco, beer, cattle, metal coins, paper bills, and checks. Money is evaluated based on how well it accomplishes the three functions of money. Money is what money does!

1. Use the following table to evaluate how well each item would perform the functions of money today. If an item seems to fulfill the function, put a + sign in the box; if it does not fulfill a function well, place a – sign in the box. Put a ? sign in the box if you are unsure whether the item fulfills that function of money. Circle the best form of money (the item with the most + signs).

Item	Medium of exchange	Store of value	Standard of value
Salt			
Cattle			
Gold	✓	✓	✓
Copper coins	✓	✓	✓
Beaver pelts			
Personal checks	✓	✓	✓
Savings account passbook		✓	✓
Prepaid phone card			
Debit card	✓	✓	✓
Credit card			
Bushels of wheat			
$1 bill	✓	✓	✓
$100 bill	✓	✓	✓

Defining and Measuring the Money Supply

Defining and measuring money is a difficult task because of changes in technology and the financial system. There is agreement on a simple conceptual definition of money. However, the complexity of the real world prevents agreement on a single measure of the money supply.

The Federal Reserve (Fed) uses *monetary* aggregates (called M0, M1, and M2) as a way to measure the money supply. In defining these measures of the money supply, the Fed draws lines between groups of assets that serve both the medium-of-exchange and store-of-value functions of money to varying degrees. Each monetary aggregate becomes broader. That is, it includes the previous category plus additional forms of money. As the categories become broader, they include less *liquid* assets. *Liquidity* refers to the ease with which an asset can be turned into cash. Cash is therefore the most liquid asset (because it is cash already!). Other assets that are included in the broader monetary aggregates are less liquid since it takes time (or a loss of value) to turn them into cash.

■ **M0** includes paper currency and coins.

■ **M1** includes M0, demand deposits, and traveler's checks.

■ **M2** includes M1, savings and small time deposits, and money market shares.

M0 and M1 include items that are primarily used as a medium of exchange while M2 adds items that are primarily used as a store of value.

In each of the following scenarios, which function of money is being served? Indicate **M** for medium of exchange, **S** for store of value, or **U** for unit of account.

_M_ 2. You pay for your lunch with a $5 bill.

_U_ 3. A car is described as being worth $5,000.

_S_ 4. A grandparent puts $200 into a savings account for a grandchild's future.

_U_ 5. You decide you want to give $10 worth of candy to a friend for his birthday.

_M_ 6. A driver pays a $2 toll.

_S_ 7. You set aside $10 per week to save up for a new computer.

8. Why are credit cards not considered money? Do they serve any of the functions of money?

9. Order the list of assets below from 1 to 5, with 1 being most liquid and 5 being least liquid.

_1_ a $10 bill   _2_ a traveler's check   _4_ a car   _3_ a money market share   _5_ a house

10. Use the data in Table 4-1.1 to calculate M0, M1, and M2. Assume all items not mentioned are zero.

Table 4-1.1
Calculating the Money Supply

Checkable deposits (demand deposits, NOW, ATM, and credit union share draft accounts)	$850
Currency	$200
Large time deposits	$800
Noncheckable savings deposits	$302
Small time deposits	$1,745
Institutional money market mutual funds	$1,210

(A) M0 = _____

(B) M1 = _____

(C) M2 = _____

The Financial System and Financial Assets

The financial system is made up of *financial markets* that facilitate the flow of funds from lenders to borrowers. In financial markets, households invest their savings in financial assets, which provide funds for investment spending. A well-functioning financial system is important to the economy because it makes households' savings available for investment that leads to long-run economic growth. The financial system helps to address three problems: transactions costs, risk, and liquidity. Financial markets reduce transaction costs by making it easier and less costly to match borrowers and lenders. They can be used to reduce the risk taken by individual lenders and borrowers by allowing *diversification* (investing in several different assets). And they can be used as a way to provide liquidity (access to cash). *Financial intermediaries* (e.g., banks and mutual funds) are institutions that transform funds they gather into financial assets.

A *financial asset* is a paper claim that entitles its buyer to future income from the seller. There are four important types of financial assets: loans, stocks, bonds, and bank deposits. A loan is an agreement to repay, with interest. A bond is an IOU issued by the borrower that represents a promise to pay fixed interest payments at regular intervals and repay the principal on a specified date. A stock is a share in the ownership of a company. A mutual fund is a financial intermediary that creates a *portfolio* (collection of financial assets) made up of different stocks and resells shares of it to individual investors. A mutual fund allows small investors to diversify their portfolio. Bank deposits are claims on a bank that oblige it to give funds back to a depositor on demand.

11. In each of the following scenarios, identify the financial asset (*loan, stock, bond, bank deposit*) and what important function of financial markets is being served (*reduce transaction costs, reduce risk, provide liquidity*). Explain how the asset is serving the function(s) you identify.

Scenario	Financial asset	Function(s)
(A) The cost of building a new factory is financed by selling shares in the company.	_____	_____
(B) Funds from many small savers are combined and provided to an individual to buy a house.	_____	_____
(C) The $1,000 in your savings account at your local bank pays you 3 percent interest.	_____	_____
(D) A firm borrows money by promising to pay a fixed sum of interest each year for 10 years and then pay back the amount borrowed at the end of 10 years.	_____	_____

Time Value of Money

A dollar you receive today is worth more than a dollar you may receive a year from today! Money has a time value because interest rates are positive. For example, if you earn 5 percent per year on your savings account, one dollar will grow to one dollar plus five cents after one year. Since the present value of $1.05 to be received one year from now (if interest rates are 5%) is $1.00, then the present value of $1.00 to be received one year from now (again if interest rates are 5%) must be some value less than $1.00. In fact, the present value can be calculated using the formula

$$PV = FV / (1 + r)^n$$

where

PV is present value

FV is future value

r is the rate of interest per period

n is the number of compounding periods (per year).

Using the formula for our example:

PV = $1.00 / $(1.05)^1$

PV = $0.95.

Today's value of $1.00 to be received one year from now if the interest rate is 5 percent is $0.95.

Business executives must consider the time value of money when making business investment spending decisions. They know that future profit projections must be converted to the present value in order to make a correct decision about whether a certain business project is profitable. Notice that the interest rate is in the denominator of the formula indicating the present value is inversely related to the interest rate. Thus, less business investment spending is worthwhile at higher interest rates.

For example, assume a business was considering the purchase of a new machine that costs $2,000 now. The machine is expected to generate profits of $1,000 at the end of year one and $1,400 at the end of year two. For simplicity, assume the machine completely wears out and is worthless after the two years. Also assume the business must borrow the $2,000 at 9 percent interest. Should the business borrow and purchase the machine?

Using the present value formula:

$$PV = \$1,000 / (1.09)^1 + \$1,400 / (1.09)^2 = \$917.43 + \$1,178.35 = \$2,095.78.$$

The business should invest in the machine since the present value of its future profits from the machine is greater than the cost of the machine: $2,095.78 − $2,000 = $95.78.

Now, what if the rate the business had to pay to borrow increased to 15 percent?

Using the present value formula:

$$PV = \$1,000 / (1.15)^1 + \$1,400 / (1.15)^2 = \$869.57 + \$1,058.60 = \$1,928.17.$$

The business should not invest in the machine since the present value of its future profits from the machine is now less than the cost of the machine: $1,928.17 − $2,000 = ($71.83).

Understanding the time value of money also helps for understanding the relationship between bond prices and interest rates. A bond is a loan with a fixed interest rate called the coupon rate. Bonds are long-term fixed-rate loans of usually 20 or 30 years. The seller (borrower) of a bond agrees to pay the buyer (lender) the amount of interest specified each year plus the face value of the bond at the end of the specified period, again typically 20 or 30 years. Often the buyer of the bond (lender) incurs a liquidity problem and needs to sell the bond before it reaches its maturity. So, at what price can the owner of the bond sell the bond?

To answer that question, let's assume the original bond was a 20-year bond with a face value of $1,000 and the coupon rate was 5 percent. That means the owner was receiving $50 in interest payments each year and was planning on receiving the $1,000 back at the end of year 20. But, let's further assume the owner needs some cash and wants to sell the bond after owning it for 18 years and that current interest rates for bonds with the same level of risk are now 7 percent. That means there are two more interest payments due (one next year and one two years from now) and the face value will be due at the date of maturity or 20th year (two years from now). What price can the owner sell the bond for now that current interest rates are higher?

Using the present value formula:

$$PV = \$50 / (1.07)^1 + \$1,050 / (1.07)^2 = \$46.73 + \$917.11 = \$963.84.$$

Note: Current interest rate is higher and the price of the bond is lower.

Now assume that current interest rates for bonds with the same level of risk are now 3 percent, which is lower than the 5 percent coupon rate. So, now what price can the owner sell the bond?

Using the present value formula:

$$PV = \$50 / (1.03)^1 + \$1,050 / (1.03)^2 = \$48.54 + \$1,019.42 = \$1,067.96.$$

Note: Current interest rate is lower and the price of the bond is higher. We can conclude that bond prices are inversely related to interest rates.

Final note: What would the same $1,000 bond sell for if interest rates were still equal to the 5 percent coupon rate? Hopefully, you concluded that the price would be the same as the original price or $1,000. To check this out using our formula:

$$PV = \$50 / (1.05)^1 + \$1,050 / (1.05)^2 = \$47.62 + \$952.38 = \$1,000.$$

1. What will $3,000 deposited into a savings account be worth after one year if interest rates are 3 percent compounded yearly?

$$3000 = \frac{FV}{(1+.03)^1}$$

$$\$3,090$$

2. What will $3,000 deposited into a savings account be worth after two years if interest rates are 3 percent compounded yearly?

3. What is the present value of $3,000 you are scheduled to receive one year from today if you are currently earning 3 percent on your savings account?

4. What is the present value of $3,000 you are scheduled to receive two years from today if you are currently earning 3 percent on your savings account?

5. Assume you have owned a 20-year $1,000 bond with a coupon rate of 6 percent for 17 years. If current interest rates on similar bonds are 9 percent, at what price could you sell the bond today?

6. Assume a business is deciding whether to invest in a new project that is projected to generate profits of $90,000 each year for the next three years. The project start-up costs are $225,000.

    (A) If the business normally earns 11 percent on its investments, should the business invest? Show/explain.

    (B) If the business normally earns 5 percent on its investments, should the business invest? Show/explain.

Banks and the Creation of Money

A bank is a financial intermediary that uses bank deposits to finance investment. That is, a bank receives deposits from savers (households) and loans them out to investors (firms). Banks earn profits by making loans. They will loan out most, but not all, of the deposits they receive. They can't loan out all of the deposits because they have to provide depositors with their funds, on demand (which is the origin of the term *demand deposits*). The fraction of deposits that a bank keeps on hand (either in their vault or deposited with the Federal Reserve) is the bank's *reserves*. Banks are required by law to keep a certain minimum fraction of their deposits on reserve. These are called *required reserves*. Any reserves in excess of the required reserves are called *excess reserves*. When banks keep only a fraction of their deposits on hand and can loan out the rest, it is called a *fractional reserve* banking system. With a fractional reserve system, banks can create money to expand the money supply.

To see how a bank can create money and increase the money supply in the economy, consider the following scenario.

1. A new checkable deposit of $1,000 is made in Bank 1. The required reserve ratio is 10 percent of checkable deposits, and banks do not hold any excess reserves. That is, banks loan out the other 90 percent of their deposits. Assume that all money loaned out by one bank is redeposited in another bank. To see how the new deposit creates money and increases the money supply, find the following values.

    (A) Bank 1 must keep required reserves = $__100__

    (B) Bank 1 can loan = $__900__

    (C) When the proceeds of the loan are redeposited, Bank 2 receives new deposits = $__900__

    (D) Bank 2 must keep additional required reserves = $__90__

    (E) Bank 2 can now make new loans = $__810__

    (F) When the proceeds of the loan are redeposited, Bank 3 receives new deposits = $__810__

    (G) Bank 3 must keep additional required reserves = $__81__

    (H) Bank 3 can now make new loans = $__729__

2. Use your answers from above to complete Table 4-3.1. Round the values to two decimals (e.g., $59.05). After you have completed the table, fill in the blanks in the statements that follow.

Table 4-3.1
Checkable Deposits, Reserves, and Loans in Seven Banks

Bank	New checkable deposits	10% required reserves	Loans
1	$1,000.00	$100.00	$900.00
2	$900.00	90.00	$810.00
3	810	$81.00	729
4	729	72.90	$656.10
5	656.10	65.61	590.49
6	590.49	$59.05	531.44
7	$531.44	53.14	$478.30
All other banks combined	4782.98	478.29	4304.67
Total for all banks	$10,000.00	1,000	$9,000.00

(A) The original deposit of $1,000 increased total bank reserves by $ 1000 . Eventually, this led to a total of $10,000 expansion of bank deposits, $ 1000 of which was because of the original deposit, while $ 9000 was because of bank lending activities.

(B) If the required reserve had been 15 percent instead of 10 percent, the amount of deposit expansion would have been *(more / (less))* than in this example.

(C) If the fractional reserve had been 5 percent instead of 10 percent, the amount of deposit expansion would have been *((more) / less)* than in this example.

(D) If banks had not loaned out all of their excess reserves, the amount of deposit expansion would have been *(more / (less))* than in this example.

(E) If all loans had not been redeposited in the banking system, the amount of deposit expansion would have been *(more / (less))* than in this example.

3. Another way to represent the multiple expansion of deposits is through *T-accounts*. A T-account shows offsetting assets and liabilities. For the bank, *assets* include loans, deposits with the Federal Reserve, and Treasury securities. *Liabilities* include deposits. Use the T-account below to show how the new $1,000 deposit described in the previous example would be listed in a T-account.

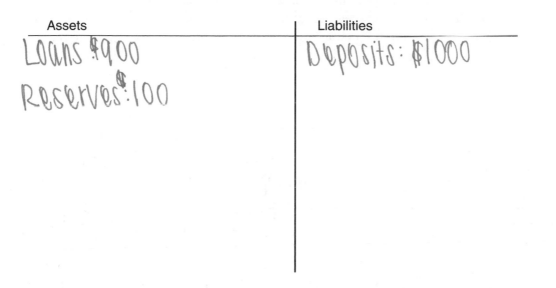

Assets	Liabilities
Loans $900	Deposits: $1000
Reserves $100	

An easier way to determine how much money can be created if the bank loans out all of its excess reserves is to use the *deposit expansion multiplier*. The deposit expansion multiplier determines how much money can be created in the economy from an initial deposit. The formula for the deposit expansion multiplier is equal to (1/rr), where rr is the reserve requirement.

Deposit expansion multiplier = 1/rr.

In this example, the reserve requirement is 10 percent so the deposit expansion multiplier is (1/0.1), which equals 10. This means that for every dollar of new excess reserves, the money supply will increase by $10.

To find the total amount of money created, use the following equation:

Expansion of the money supply = excess reserves × multiplier.

The multiplier is 10, and excess reserves from the initial bank deposit are $900. So the potential expansion of money (M1) would be $900 times 10, or $9,000. M1 now consists of the new deposit of $1,000 plus the $9,000 created.

⚠ *Student Alert:* Make sure you read any money multiplier questions carefully to determine exactly which value the question asks for. For example, does it ask you to calculate the initial change or the final change?

4. Assume that $1,000 is deposited in the bank, and that each bank loans out all of its excess reserves. For each of the following required reserve ratios, calculate the amount that the bank must hold in required reserves, the amount that will be excess reserves, the deposit expansion multiplier, and the maximum amount that the money supply could increase.

	Required reserve ratio		
	1%	5%	10%
Required reserves	10	50	100
Excess reserves	990	950	900
Deposit expansion multiplier	100	20	10
Maximum increase in the money supply	99,000	19000	9,000

(A) Will an increase in the reserve requirement increase or decrease the money supply? Explain.

decrease bc cant loan out so much money and create money

(B) What will happen to deposits, required reserves, excess reserves, and the money supply if deposits are withdrawn from the banking system?

deposits↓ rr↓ excess reserves↓ money supply↓

(C) What could happen at each stage of the money creation process to prevent the money supply from increasing the full amount predicted by the deposit expansion multiplier?

The Money Market

The quantity of money (e.g., M1) is determined by the Federal Reserve (the Fed) through its control of the reserve requirement and money creation by the banking system. The price of money is the interest rate. The interest rate is the price of money because it is what borrowers must pay to obtain money and it is also the opportunity cost of holding money rather than loaning it out.

The money market consists of the demand for money (MD) and the supply of money (MS). The Fed determines the quantity of money supplied. Since it is determined by the Fed, the money supply is independent of the interest rate, and the money supply curve is a vertical line.

The demand for money is based on a decision by consumers to hold wealth in the form of interest-bearing assets (e.g. savings accounts) or as money (noninterest-bearing). There are three types of money demand, based on the three basic motives people have for holding money (rather than interest-bearing assets).

■ Transactions demand — to make purchases of goods and services

■ Precautionary demand — to serve as protection against an unexpected need

■ Speculative demand — to serve as a store of wealth

The demand for money is a function of interest rates and income. The interest rate is the opportunity cost of holding money because it represents the forgone interest income that was given up in order to hold money. The demand for money has an inverse relationship with the interest rate. As the interest rate increases, the opportunity cost of holding money increases and people hold less money. As the interest rate falls, the opportunity cost of holding money falls and people hold more money. The negatively sloped demand curve for money represents the quantity of money demanded at various interest rates.

Figure 4-4.1
The Money Market

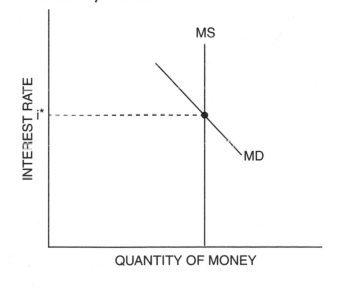

1. Now suppose there is an increase in the money supply. Show the change in the money supply and the resulting change in the equilibrium interest rate on Figure 4-4.1 What happens to the quantity of money demanded when the interest rate changes? What happens to the quantity of loans as the interest rate changes? Explain.

2. Now draw a new graph of the money market, illustrating the equilibrium interest rate.

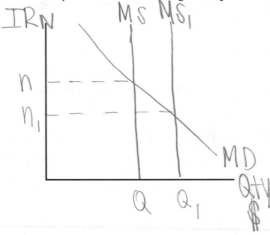

3. Suppose the demand for money increases. Show the change in money demand and the resulting interest rate on your graph. What happens to the quantity of loans as the interest rate changes? Explain.

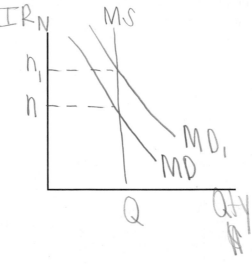

The Loanable Funds Market

The loanable funds market is made up of borrowers, who demand funds (D_{lf}), and lenders, who supply funds (S_{lf}). The loanable funds market determines the real interest rate (the price of loans), as shown in Figure 4-5.1.

Figure 4-5.1
Market for Loanable Funds

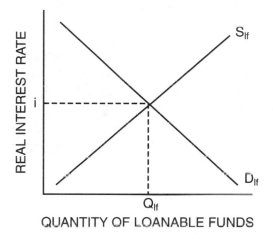

Four groups demand and supply loanable funds: consumers, the government, foreigners, and businesses. The same four groups demand and supply loanable funds, so it is important to understand the economic behavior depicted by the demand and supply curves for loanable funds.

The demand curve for loanable funds is negatively sloped. More loans are demanded at lower real interest rates, and fewer loans are demanded when real interest rates are higher. Businesses, for example, will find more projects worthwhile to invest in at lower rates than at higher rates. Profits rise as interest rates fall. Businesses will therefore borrow more at lower rates to finance the increased business investment spending. Consumer and foreigner borrowing is also sensitive to changes in the interest rate. Consider that the monthly payments for a mortgage are higher with a higher real interest rate. As the rate rises, fewer consumers can afford the higher mortgage payments. Government borrowing is not very sensitive to the interest rate.

The upward slope of the supply of the loanable funds demonstrates the willingness of households to save. The opportunity cost of saving is spending now. The more income saved, the less can be spent now. The opportunity cost rises as more and more income is saved. Thus higher rates of interest are needed to compensate for the increasing opportunity cost of saving.

The equilibrium real interest rate is the rate at which the total amount savers are willing to lend equals the total amount borrowers are willing to borrow. The major determinants of the demand for loanable funds are business confidence and expectations, consumer confidence and expectations, government budget plans, and income levels.

For example, if businesses are confident of future profits, they will want to borrow more at all possible real interest rates to expand operations, and the D_{lf} curve shifts to the right. If the government decreases spending to reduce the deficit it decreases the need to borrow, and the D_{lf} curve shifts to the left. If consumers become concerned that the economy is heading toward a recession, they will become concerned about their ability to repay loans and will cut back on their borrowing, decreasing the demand for loanable funds. On the other hand, rising incomes would cause consumers to borrow more since their higher incomes enable them to pay back higher amounts.

On the supply side, if the government reduces the income tax rate on interest income, consumers will want to save more at every real interest rate, and the S_{lf} curve will shift to the right. Anything that causes consumers to save more will shift the S_{lf} curve to the right. The Federal Reserve plays a significant role on the supply side of the loanable funds market.

A good way to view the loanable funds market is to consider the bond market with an understanding that bonds are fixed-rate loans. Thus, anyone who buys a newly issued bond is loaning funds to the seller of the bond. The demand for loanable funds then is the same as the supply of bonds in the bond market, and the supply of loanable funds is the same as the demand for bonds in the bond market. Considering these relationships helps to understand that bond prices and interest rates are inversely related. For example, an increase in demand for loanable funds (increase in supply of bonds) raises interest rates in the loanable funds market (and decreases bond prices in the bond market).

🛑 *Student Alert:* **Make sure you understand the differences (and similarities) between the money market and the loanable funds market and use the appropriate one! The slope of the supply curve is a key distinction!**

1. Explain why the demand for loanable funds is negatively sloped. (Use the business borrower in your explanation.)

2. Explain why the supply of loanable funds is positively sloped. (Use household savers in your explanation.)

3. Is the interest rate in the loanable funds market nominal or real? Explain.

4. Draw a graph of the loanable funds market showing the effect of each of the following on the real interest rate and quantity of loanable funds.

   (A) The government increases spending *ceteris paribus*.

   (B) The government increases tax on income from interest payments.

   (C) The Federal Reserve buys bonds on the open market facilitating an increase of the money supply.

(D) The University of Michigan releases the index of consumer and business confidence, which indicates both are lower.

(E) Consumers in China decide to increase consumption.

The Federal Reserve and Central Banking

The Federal Reserve System is the central bank of the United States. A central bank is an institution that oversees and regulates the banking system and controls the money supply. The Federal Reserve System (known as "the Fed") is made up of 12 privately owned District Federal Reserve Banks and a federal government agency that oversees the system, called the Board of Governors. The Fed has four basic functions:

1. Provide financial services for commercial banks (like holding reserves, providing cash, and clearing checks)

2. Supervise and regulate banking institutions to ensure the safety and soundness of the nation's banking and financial system

3. Maintain stability of the financial system by providing liquidity to financial institutions in order to maintain their safety and soundness

4. Conduct monetary policy to prevent or address extreme fluctuations in the economy

The Fed's goal is "to promote effectively the goals of maximum employment, stable prices and moderate long-term interest rates." A primary goal of the Fed is to stabilize prices, which is arguably the strongest contribution the Fed can make to promoting economic growth. Over time, it has become evident that monetary policy's long-term influence over prices is strong but its influence over real output and real interest rates is mostly short term.

To promote employment and price stability, the Fed can use monetary policy to raise or lower interest rates through the money market. Lower interest rates promote spending and investment that leads to increased employment (this is called *expansionary* monetary policy). Higher interest rates prevent inflation and promote price stability (this is called *contractionary* monetary policy).

The Fed has three main policy tools it can use to control equilibrium interest rates in the money market: the reserve requirement, the discount rate, and open-market operations.

1. **The reserve requirement.** The Fed sets the percentages of bank deposits that must be held as reserves. Greater excess reserves lead banks to expand credit, which expands the money supply. Fewer excess reserves lead banks to reduce credit, which decreases the money supply. Changes in the money supply change equilibrium interest rates in the money market. Because changes in the reserve requirement can have powerful impacts, the reserve requirement is seldom used as a tool of monetary policy.

2. **The discount rate.** The discount rate is the rate that commercial banks must pay to borrow from the Fed. When it is cheaper to borrow from the Fed, banks will borrow more reserves; when it is more expensive to borrow from the Fed, banks will borrow less. More reserves lead banks to expand credit, which expands the money supply. Fewer reserves lead banks to reduce credit, which reduces the money supply. The discount rate is set by the Fed, generally a percentage point above *the federal funds rate* (which is the interest rate banks charge each other for overnight loans).

The equilibrium federal funds rate established in the money market is the focus of monetary policy, not the discount rate set directly by the Fed.

3. **Open market operations (OMOs).** OMOs refers to the Fed buying and selling U.S. Treasury bills, normally through a transaction with commercial banks that changes the banks' reserves. When the Fed buys Treasury bills, it increases the banks' reserves, and when the Fed sells Treasury bills, it decreases the banks' reserves. The change in the banks' reserves leads to a change in the money supply. Changes in the money supply change equilibrium interest rates in the money market. OMOs are the most frequently used monetary policy tool.

Student Alert: **Open market operations include buying and selling government bonds. When you are asked about an open market operation, you should answer in terms of buying bonds or selling bonds.**

The Mechanics of Monetary Policy

To manage the money supply, the Fed uses the tools of monetary policy to influence the quantity of reserves in the banking system. The following examples use T-accounts to show how the Fed could use open market operations to increase the money supply by $100.

Figure 4-6.1 shows T-accounts for the economy. The required reserve ratio is 10 percent. The bank holds $26 in reserve accounts and $4 in Federal Reserve notes (vault cash). Total bank reserves equal $30, so total reserves equal required reserves and there are no excess reserves. Net worth = assets – liabilities.

Figure 4-6.1
T-Accounts

Assets			Liabilities
	The Fed		
Treasury securities	$83	$26	Reserve accounts of banks
		$57	Federal Reserve notes
	Banks		
Reserve accounts	$26	$300	Checkable deposits
Federal Reserve notes	$4		
Loans	$405	$135	Net worth (to stockholders)
	Bank customers		
Checkable deposits	$300	$405	Loans
Federal Reserve notes	$53		
Treasury securities	$52		
	Money supply = $353 ($300 + $53)		

Expansionary Policy via Open Market Purchases

Now suppose the Fed believes the economy is heading into a recession and wishes to increase the money supply by $100, so it uses open market operations and purchases $10 worth of Treasury securities from the public.

   Figure 4-6.2 shows the T-accounts after the effects of the Fed action work their way through the economy. Compare Figure 4-6.1 with Figure 4-6.2. The Fed's $10 increase in reserve accounts yields a $100 increase in the money supply.

 Figure 4-6.2

T-Accounts after $10 Open Market Purchase

Assets			Liabilities
The Fed			
Treasury securities (+$10)	$93	$36	Reserve accounts of banks (+$10)
		$57	Federal Reserve notes
Banks			
Reserve accounts (+$10)	$36	$400	Checkable deposits (+$100)
Federal Reserve notes	$4		
Loans (+$90)	$495	$135	Net worth (to stockholders)
Bank customers			
Checkable deposits (+$100)	$400	$495	Loans (+$90)
Federal Reserve notes	$53		
Treasury securities (−$10)	$42		
Money supply = $453 ($400 + $53)			

   For the following questions, start with the T-accounts in Figure 4-6.1. Suppose the Fed wishes to *decrease* the money supply from $353 to $303 by open market operations. The reserve requirement is 10 percent.

1. Will the Fed want to buy or sell existing Treasury securities? _Sell_   50

2. What is the money multiplier? _10_

3. What is the value of Treasury securities that need to be bought or sold? _$5_

4. Fill in Figure 4-6.3 to show the accounts after open market operations are finished and all changes have worked their way through the economy.

Figure 4-6.3

T-Accounts after Open Market Operations Are Finished

Assets	Liabilities
The Fed	
Treasury securities	Reserve accounts of banks
$57	Federal Reserve notes
Banks	
Reserve accounts	Checkable deposits
Federal Reserve notes	
Loans $135	Net worth (to stockholders)
Bank customers	
Checkable deposits	Loans
Federal Reserve notes $53	
Treasury securities	

Money supply = _____

For the following questions, suppose banks keep zero excess reserves and the reserve requirement is 15 percent.

5. What is the deposit expansion multiplier? __6.67__

6. A customer deposits $100,000 in a checking account.

(A) How much must the bank add to its reserves? __15000__

(B) How much of this can the bank lend to new customers? __85,000__

(C) In what two forms can a bank hold the new required reserves? _____

7. Suppose that the $100,000 had previously been held in Federal Reserve notes under the customer's mattress and that banks continue to hold no excess reserves. By how much will the customer's deposit cause the money supply to grow? 566,950

$85,000 \times 6.67$

8. Circle the correct symbol in Table 4-6.1.

 Table 4-6.1

Fed Actions and Their Effects

Federal Reserve action	Bank reserves	Money supply	Fed funds rate
(A) Sold Treasury securities on the open market	↑ (↓)	↑ (↓)	(↑) ↓
(B) Bought Treasury securities on the open market	(↑) ↓	(↑) ↓	↑ (↓)
(C) Raised the discount rate	↑ (↓)	↑ (↓)	(↑) ↓
(D) Lowered the discount rate	(↑) ↓	(↑) ↓	↑ (↓)
(E) Raised the reserve requirement	↑ (↓)	↑ (↓)	(↑) ↓
(F) Lowered the reserve requirement	(↑) ↓	(↑) ↓	↑ (↓)

(handwritten in left margin: contractionary, expansionary, contract expansion, contract expansion)

9. In Table 4-6.2, indicate how the Fed could use each of the three monetary policy tools to pursue an expansionary policy and a contractionary policy.

Table 4-6.2

Tools of Monetary Policy

Monetary policy	Expansionary policy	Contractionary policy
(A) Open market opeations	buy treasury securities	sell
(B) Discount rate	lower discount rate	raise
(C) Reserve requirements	lower rr	raise rr

Monetary Policy

Monetary policy is the action of the Federal Reserve (the Fed) to prevent or address extreme economic fluctuations. The Fed uses its monetary policy tools to influence equilibrium interest rates in the money market through its control of bank reserves. The Fed lowers interest rates through expansionary monetary policy to prevent or address recessions, and it raises interest rates through contractionary monetary policy to prevent or address inflation. Monetary policy is transmitted to the economy through changes in aggregate demand. Monetary policy will have both short-run and long-run effects in the economy. In the following figures, long-run aggregate supply, short-run aggregate supply, and demand curves are represented by LRAS, SRAS, and AD.

Figure 4-7.1
Effects of Monetary Policy in the Economy (Recession)

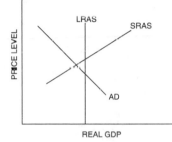

1. Suppose that initially the economy is at the intersection of AD and SRAS in Figure 4-7.1.

    (A) What monetary policy can the Fed implement to move the economy to full-employment?

    expansionary

    (B) If the Fed is going to use open market operations, it should (*buy* / *sell*) Treasury securities.

    (C) The effect will (*increase* / *decrease*) Treasury security (bond) prices.

    Bond & interest rates have an inverse relationship

    (D) In the short run, what is the effect on nominal interest rates? Explain.

    Fall → Real GDP

    (E) In the short run, what happens to real output? Shift the curve on the graph to show how the Fed's action results in a change in real output and explain why the shift occurs.

    increase

    (F) In the short run, what happens to the price level? Explain how the Fed's action results in a change to the price level.

    increase

Figure 4-7.2
Effects of Monetary Policy in the Economy (Inflation)

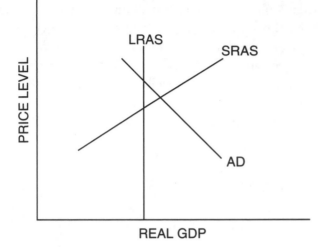

2. Suppose that initially the economy is at the intersection of AD and SRAS in Figure 4-7.2.

   (A) What monetary policy can the Fed implement to move the economy to full-employment?

   contractionary

   (B) If the Fed is going to use open market operations, it should (*buy* / *sell*) Treasury securities.

   (C) The effect will (*increase* / *decrease*) Treasury security (bond) prices.

   (D) In the short run, what is the effect on nominal interest rates? Explain.

   increase

   (E) In the short run, what happens to real output? Shift the curve on the graph to show how the Fed's action results in a change in real output and explain why the shift occurs.

   decline

   (F) In the short run, what happens to the price level? Explain how the Fed's action results in a change to the price level.

   decrease

3. In the situation shown in Figure 4-7.3, suppose that the monetary authorities decide to maintain the level of employment represented by the output level Y_1 by using expansionary monetary policy.

Figure 4-7.3
Monetary Policy in the Long Run

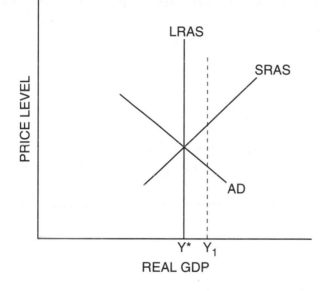

(A) Explain the effect of the expansionary monetary policy on the price level and output in the short run. *Expand* *increase*

(B) Explain the effect on the price level and output in the long run. *SRAS shifts left GDPrↆ PLↆ*

(C) Explain what you think will happen to the nominal rate of interest and the real rate of interest in the short run as the Fed continues to increase the money supply. Explain why. *decrease*

(D) Explain what you think will happen to the nominal rate of interest and the real rate of interest in the long run. Explain why. *increases*

4. Many economists think that moving from short-run equilibrium to long-run equilibrium may take several years. List three reasons why the economy might not immediately move to long-run equilibrium.

5. Briefly summarize the long-run impact of an expansionary monetary policy on the economy.

output does not increase
pl↑

Figure 4-7.4
Expansionary Monetary Policy

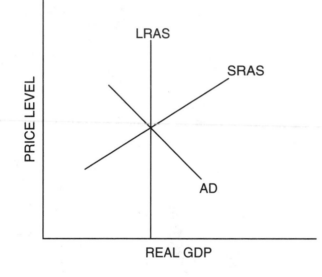

6. Suppose that initially the economy is at the intersection of AD and SRAS as shown in Figure 4-7.4. Now, the Fed decides to implement expansionary monetary policy to increase the level of employment.

(A) In the short run, what happens to real output? Explain why.

↑

(B) In the short run, what happens to the price level? Explain why.

↑

(C) In the short run, what happens to employment and nominal wages? Explain why.

↑ stay the same (stick wages)

(D) In the short run, what happens to nominal interest rates and real interest rates?

↓   ↓

(E) In the long run, what happens to real output? Explain why.

↓

(F) In the long run, what happens to the price level? Explain why.

(G) In the long run, what happens to employment and nominal wages? Explain why.

(H) In the long run, what happens to the nominal interest rate and the real interest rate?

The Quantity Theory of Money

The relationship among money, price, and real output can be represented by the *equation of exchange*, which typically takes the following form:

$$MV = PQ$$

where

M = the money supply
V = the velocity of money (the number of times an average dollar bill is spent)
P = the average price level
Q = real value of all final goods and services (real gross domestic product [GDP])

This equation shows the balance between "money," represented on the left side of the equation, and goods and services, represented on the right side of the equation. The equation shows that, for a given level of V, if M increases more than Q there must be an increase in P (inflation) to keep the two sides of the equation equal. This means that an increase in the money supply not offset by an increase in real output will lead to inflation. Classical economists assumed that the velocity of money was stable (constant) over time because institutional factors—such as how frequently people are paid—largely determine velocity. Therefore, changes in the money supply will lead to inflation if the economy is at full employment.

1. Define (in your own words and in one or two sentences each) the four variables in the equation of exchange. *from above*

2. The product of V and M equals PQ. What is PQ?

   PQ is the average price level times the reale value of all final goods and services

3. Suppose velocity remains constant, while the money supply increases. Explain how this would affect nominal GDP. *the nominal GDP would increase because the money supply increases*

4. Changes in technology have led to increases in electronic transactions. Explain how these changes affect velocity. *velocity increases.*

Real versus Nominal Interest Rates

If you bought a one-year bond for $1,000 and the bond paid an interest rate of 10 percent, at the end of the year would you be 10 percent wealthier? You will certainly have 10 percent more money than you did a year earlier, but can you buy 10 percent more? If the price level has risen, the answer is that you cannot buy 10 percent more. If the inflation rate were 8 percent, then you could buy only 2 percent more; if the inflation rate were 12 percent, you would be able to buy 2 percent less! The *nominal interest rate* is the rate the bank pays you on your savings or the rate that appears on your bond or car loan. The *real interest rate* represents the change in your purchasing power. The *expected real interest rate* represents the amount you need to receive in real terms to forgo consumption now for consumption in the future.

The *Fisher Equation* shows the relationship between the nominal interest rate, the real interest rate, and the inflation rate as shown below:

$$r = i - \pi$$

where

r = the real interest rate

i = the nominal interest rate

π = the inflation rate.

In the previous example with the 10 percent bond, if the inflation rate were 6 percent, then your real interest rate (the increase in your purchasing power) would be 4 percent ($6 = 10 - 4$).

Obviously banks and customers do not know what inflation is going to be, so the interest rates on loans, bonds, and so forth are set based on expected inflation. The expected real interest rate is

$$re - i - \pi e$$

where

πe = the expected inflation rate.

The equation can be rewritten as $i = re + \pi e$.

A bank sets the nominal interest rate equal to its expected real interest rate plus the expected inflation rate. However, the real interest rate it actually receives may be different if inflation is not equal to the bank's expected inflation rate.

According to the Fisher Equation, if the Federal Reserve increases the money supply, the price level will increase. The resulting inflation will increase the nominal interest rate, decrease the real interest rate, or some combination of the two. This is known as the *Fisher Effect*. In the short run, increases in the money supply decrease the nominal interest rate and real interest rate. In the long run, an increase in the money supply will result in an increase in the price level and the nominal interest rate.

Table 4-9.1
Real and Nominal Interest Rates

Year	Nominal interest rate (%)	Inflation rate (%)	Real interest rate (%)
1	5.02	1.87	
2	5.07	1.85	
3	4.78	1.14	
4	4.64	1.56	
5	5.82	2.29	
6	3.39	1.95	

1. Table 4-9.1 provides the nominal interest rates and inflation rates for the Years 1–6. Compute the real interest rates and then graph the nominal and real interest rates on Figure 4-9.1.

Figure 4-9.1
Real and Nominal Interest Rates

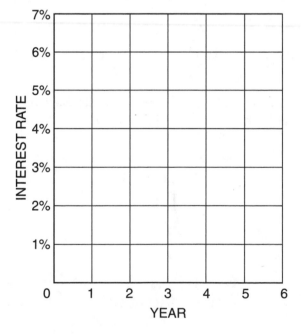

Advanced Placement Economics Macroeconomics: Student Resource Manual © Council for Economic Education, New York, N.Y.

Circle the letter of each correct answer.

1. The M0 definition of money includes which of the following?

   (A) Currency

   (B) Demand deposits

   (C) Savings accounts

   (D) Small time deposits

   (E) Money market accounts

2. If the legal reserve requirement is 25 percent, the value of the simple deposit expansion multiplier is

   (A) 2.

   (B) 4.

   (C) 5.

   (D) 10.

   (E) 1.0.

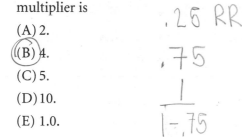

.25 RR

.75

$\frac{1}{1-.75}$

3. When money is used as a standard of value, a person is

   (A) earning more money than before.

   (B) purchasing a necessity.

   (C) making a financial transaction.

   (D) making price comparisons among products.

   (E) writing a check for groceries.

4. Which of the following are true statements about the federal funds rate?

   I. It is the same thing as the discount rate.

   II. It is the interest rate that banks charge each other for short-term loans.

   III. It is influenced by open market operations.

   (A) I only

   (B) II only

   (C) III only

   (D) I and II only

   (E) II and III only

5. Suppose the Federal Reserve buys $400,000 worth of securities from the securities dealers on the open market. If the reserve requirement is 20 percent and the banks hold no excess reserves, what will happen to the total money supply?

   (A) It will be unchanged.

   (B) It will contract by $2,000,000.

   (C) It will contract by $800,000.

   (D) It will expand by $2,000,000.

   (E) It will expand by $800,000.

6. All of the following are financial assets *except*

   (A) loans.

   (B) stocks.

   (C) bonds.

   (D) bank deposits.

   (E) required reserves.

7. A commercial bank holds $500,000 in demand deposit liabilities and $120,000 in reserves. If the required reserve ratio is 20 percent, which of the following is the maximum amount by which this single commercial bank and the maximum amount by which the banking system can increase loans?

	Amount created by single bank	Amount created by banking system
(A)	$5,000	$25,000
(B)	$20,000	$80,000
(C)	$20,000	$100,000
(D)	$30,000	$150,000
(E)	$120,000	$500,000

8. Which of the following does the Federal Reserve use most often to combat a recession?

   (A) Selling securities

   (B) Buying securities

   (C) Reducing the reserve requirement

   (D) Increasing the discount rate

   (E) Increasing the federal funds rate

9. To reduce inflation, the Federal Reserve could

   (A) expand the money supply in order to raise interest rates, which increases investment.

   (B) expand the money supply in order to lower interest rates, which increases investment.

   (C) contract the money supply in order to lower interest rates, which increases investment.

   (D) contract the money supply in order to raise interest rates, which decreases investment.

   (E) buy bonds and decrease the discount rate to encourage borrowing.

10. Reserves, the money supply, and interest rates are most likely to change in which of the following ways when the Federal Reserve sells bonds?

	Reserves	Money supply	Interest rates
(A)	Increase	Increase	Increase
(B)	Increase	Increase	Decrease
(C)	Decrease	Increase	Decrease
(D)	Decrease	Decrease	Increase
(E)	Decrease	Decrease	Decrease

11. Which of the following actions by the Federal Reserve will result in an increase in banks' excess reserves?

   (A) Buying bonds on the open market

   (B) Selling bonds on the open market

   (C) Increasing the discount rate

   (D) Increasing the reserve requirement

   (E) Increasing the federal funds rate

12. Aggregate demand and aggregate supply analysis suggests that, in the short run, an expansionary monetary policy will shift

   (A) the aggregate demand curve to the left.

   (B) the aggregate supply curve to the left.

   (C) the aggregate demand curve to the right.

   (D) the aggregate supply curve to the right.

   (E) both the aggregate demand and supply curves to the left.

13. Which of the following combinations of monetary policy actions would definitely cause a decrease in aggregate demand?

	Discount rate	Open market operations	Reserve requirement
(A)	Decrease	Buy bonds	Decrease
(B)	Decrease	Sells bonds	Decrease
(C)	Increase	Buy bonds	Increase
(D)	Increase	Sells bonds	Decrease
(E)	Increase	Sells bonds	Increase

14. A decrease in the mortgage rate will cause which of the following to happen in the loanable funds market?

   (A) Demand will increase.

   (B) Demand will decrease.

   (C) Supply will increase.

   (D) Supply will decrease.

   (E) The equilibrium interest rate will fall.

15. What will happen to the supply of loanable funds and the equilibrium interest rate if the Federal Reserve buys government securities?

	Supply	Interest rate
(A)	Increase	Increase
(B)	Increase	Decrease
(C)	Decrease	Decrease
(D)	Decrease	Decrease
(E)	Decrease	Remain unchanged

16. The real interest rate is simply stated as the

    (A) price of borrowed money in the future.

    (B) inflation rate minus the CPI.

    (C) nominal interest rate over time.

    → (D) nominal interest rate minus the expected inflation rate.

    (E) nominal interest rate plus the expected inflation rate.

17. What is the present value of $110 paid one year from now if the interest rate is 10 percent?

    (A) $121

    (B) $110

    (C) $100

    (D) $99

    (E) $11

18. The neutrality of money refers to the situation where

    (A) money has not been the cause of war.

    (B) increases in interest rates are matched by decreases in the price of bonds.

    (C) increases in interest rates are matched by increases in the price of bonds.

    → (D) increases in the money supply eventually result in no change in real output.

    (E) decreases in the money supply result in increases in the interest rate in the short run.

19. Expansionary monetary policy results in which of the following in the short run?

    I.   The money supply increases.

    II. The nominal interest rate decreases.

    III. The real interest rate decreases.

    IV. Bond prices decrease.

    (A) I and II only

    → (B) I, II, and III only

    (C) I, II, and IV only

    (D) III and IV only

    (E) IV only

20. GDP is represented in the equation of exchange as

    (A) Q.

    (B) PQ.

    (C) MV.

    (D) V.

    (E) PQ/V.

MACROECONOMICS

Inflation, Unemployment, and Stabilization Policies

Unit 5

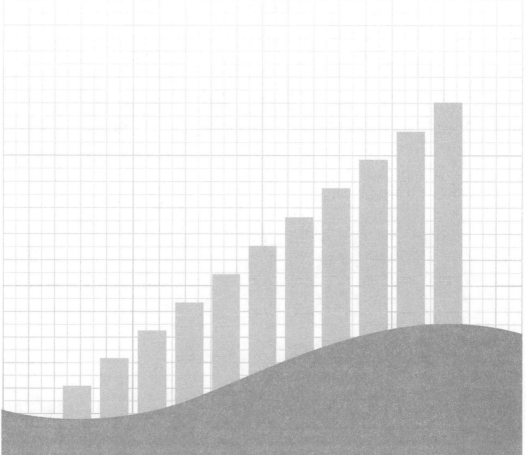

■ In the short run, equilibrium levels of GDP can occur at less than, greater than, or equal to the full-employment level of GDP. The long-run equilibrium can occur only at full employment.

■ Fiscal policy consists of government actions to increase or decrease aggregate demand. These actions involve changes in government expenditures and taxation.

■ Macroeconomic policy includes both fiscal and monetary policy. Both monetary and fiscal policies are primarily aggregate demand policies. Other economic policies are used to affect aggregate supply.

■ The government uses a contractionary fiscal policy to decrease aggregate demand when there are inflationary pressures in the economy. The government may increase taxes, decrease spending, or do a combination of the two.

■ The government uses an expansionary fiscal policy to increase aggregate demand during a recession. The government may decrease taxes, increase spending, or do a combination of the two.

■ Discretionary fiscal policy means the federal government must take deliberate action or pass a new law changing taxes or spending. The automatic or built-in stabilizers change government spending or taxes without new laws being passed or deliberate action being taken.

■ Fiscal policy that changes taxes or government spending will affect the government's budget. When the government spends more than it taxes in a year, it creates a budget deficit. When the government taxes more than it spends in a year, it creates a budget surplus. The summation of the budget deficits and surpluses over time is the national debt. Deficits and debt have an effect on the macroeconomy.

■ Crowding out is the effect on investment and consumption spending of an increase in interest rates caused by increased borrowing by the federal government. The higher interest rates crowd out business and consumer borrowing.

■ A Phillips curve illustrates the trade-off between inflation and unemployment. The trade-off differs in the short and long run, varies at different times, and is often different for increases and decreases in output.

■ The short-run Phillips curve shows a trade-off between the inflation rate and the unemployment rate. There is no trade-off between inflation and unemployment in the long run. The long-run Phillips curve is vertical.

The Tools of Fiscal Policy

Changes in taxes and government spending designed to affect the level of aggregate demand in the economy are called *fiscal policy*.

Recall that *aggregate demand* is the total amount of spending on goods and services in the economy during a stated period of time and is made up of consumer spending (C), investment (I), government spending (G), and net exports (Xn). *Aggregate supply* is the total amount of goods and services available in the economy.

During a recession, the short-run equilibrium is below the full-employment level of output. Aggregate demand is too low to bring about full employment of resources. Government can increase aggregate demand by spending more and/or cutting taxes. Increasing aggregate demand to move the economy toward full employment is *expansionary fiscal policy*. Expansionary fiscal policy increases employment but also can raise the price level and result in budget deficits.

If the level of aggregate demand is too high, it creates inflationary pressures. Government can decrease aggregate demand by reducing spending and/or increasing taxes. Decreasing aggregate demand to decrease inflationary pressures is *contractionary fiscal policy*. Contractionary fiscal policy reduces inflationary pressures but can also decrease output and employment. Contractionary fiscal policy can result in budget surpluses (or smaller budget deficits).

⊙ *Student Alert:* **Remember that the multiplier is different for taxes and for spending!**

Decide whether each of the following fiscal policies of the federal government is expansionary or contractionary. Write *expansionary* or *contractionary*, and explain the reasons for your choice.

1. The government cuts business and personal income taxes and increases its own spending.

2. The government increases the personal income tax, Social Security tax, and corporate income tax. Government spending stays the same.

3. Government spending goes up while taxes remain the same.

4. The government reduces the wages of its employees while raising taxes on consumers and businesses. Other government spending remains the same.

Effects of Fiscal Policy

Test your understanding of fiscal policy by completing Table 5-1.1. Your choices for each situation must be consistent—that is, you should choose either an expansionary or contractionary fiscal policy. (Fiscal policy cannot provide a solution to one of the situations.) Fill in the spaces as follows:

Column A: Objective for aggregate demand

Draw an up arrow to increase aggregate demand or a down arrow to decrease aggregate demand.

Column B: Action on taxes

Draw an up arrow to increase taxes or a down arrow to decrease taxes.

Column C: Action on government spending

Draw an up arrow to increase government spending or a down arrow to decrease government spending.

Column D: Effect on federal budget

Write *toward deficit* if your action will increase the deficit (or reduce the surplus) or *toward surplus* if your action will reduce the deficit (or increase the surplus).

Column E: Effect on national bebt

Draw an up arrow if your action will increase the national debt or a down arrow if your action will decrease the national debt.

Table 5-1.1
Effects of Fiscal Policy

	(A) Objective for aggregate demand	(B) Action on taxes	(C) Action on government spending	(D) Effect on federal budget	(E) Effect on national debt
1. National unemployment rate rises to 12 percent.					
2. Inflation is strong at a rate of 14 percent per year.					
3. Surverys show consumers are losing confidence in the economy, retail sales are weak, and business inventories are increasing rapidly.					
4. Business sales and investment are expanding rapidly, and economists think strong inflation lies ahead.					
5. Inflation persists while unemployment stays high.					

Discretionary Fiscal Policy and Automatic Stabilizers

One of the goals of economic policy is to stabilize the economy. This means promoting full employment and stable prices. To accomplish this, aggregate demand must be near the full-employment level of output. If aggregate demand is too low, there will be unemployment. If aggregate demand is too high, there will be inflation.

If aggregate demand is too low, government can use fiscal policy to stimulate the economy through increased spending or decreased taxes. These policies are examples of *expansionary fiscal policy*. If government wants to decrease aggregate demand, it can pursue a *contractionary fiscal policy* by decreasing taxes or increasing spending.

If government has to pass a law or take some other specific action to change taxes or spending, then the action is at the government's discretion and the policy is *discretionary policy*. If the effect happens automatically as the economic situation changes, then the policy is the result of an *automatic stabilizer*. An example of an automatic stabilizer is unemployment compensation. If the economy goes into a recession, some people are laid off and are eligible to receive unemployment compensation. The payment creates income and spending to keep aggregate demand from falling as much as it would have. Unemployment compensation stabilizes the economy automatically during a recession.

For each of the scenarios on the following page, indicate whether it represents an automatic (A) or discretionary (D) stabilizer, and whether it is an example of expansionary (E) or contractionary (C) fiscal policy.

Economic scenarios	Automatic (A) or Discretionary (D)	Expansionary (E) or Contractionary (C)
Example: Recession raises amount of unemployment compensation.	A	E
1. The government cuts personal income tax rates.		
2. The government eliminates favorable tax treatment on long-term capital gains.		
3. Incomes rise; as a result, people pay a larger fraction of their income in taxes.		
4. As a result of a recession, more families qualify for food stamps and welfare benefits.		

Economic scenarios	Automatic (A) or Discretionary (D)	Expansionary (E) or Contractionary (C)
5. The government eliminates the deductibility of interest expense for tax purposes.	_____	_____
6. The government launches a major new space program to explore Mars.	_____	_____
7. The government raises Social Security taxes.	_____	_____
8. Corporate profits increase; as a result, government collects more corporate income taxes.	_____	_____
9. The government raises corporate income tax rates.	_____	_____
10. The government gives all its employees a large pay raise.	_____	_____

Monetary and Fiscal Policy

Tools of Monetary and Fiscal Policy

Both monetary and fiscal policy can be used to influence the inflation rate and real output. In Table 5-3.1, use ↑ or ↓ to indicate what effect each specific policy has on inflation and real output in the short run.

Table 5-3.1
Monetary Policy

Monetary policy	Price level	Real output
1. Raise the federal funds rate		
2. Decrease the discount rate		
3. Decrease reserve requirement		

Fiscal policy	Price level	Real output
4. Increase government spending		
5. Increase taxes		

Policy Effects on Aggregate Supply

Fiscal and monetary policy affect the economy through changes in aggregate demand (AD). There are also policies that can affect the short-run aggregate supply (SRAS) and long-run aggregate supply (LRAS). Any policy that changes a determinant of SRAS or leads to long-run economic growth will affect the macroeconomy through the supply side. The determinants of SRAS include changes in economy-wide input prices (like wages and the price of oil) and productivity. Factors that affect the LRAS include increases in available resources, higher quality resources, or technological advances.

1. Assume the government grants businesses a substantial tax credit on capital investment. Circle the correct symbol (↑ for increase, ↓ for decrease) to indicate what will happen to the following as a result of the tax credit.

   (A) Capital investment   ↑   ↓

   (B) AD   ↑   ↓

   (C) The amount of capital available to labor   ↑   ↓

   (D) Productivity   ↑   ↓

   (E) Firms' unit cost of production   ↑   ↓

   (F) SRAS   ↑   ↓

   (G) LRAS   ↑   ↓

   (H) Real gross domestic product (GDP)   ↑   ↓

2. How will a decrease in business taxes affect firms' per unit costs?

3. Use the AS/AD diagram below to show the effect of a decrease in business taxes on SRAS, real GDP, and the price level.

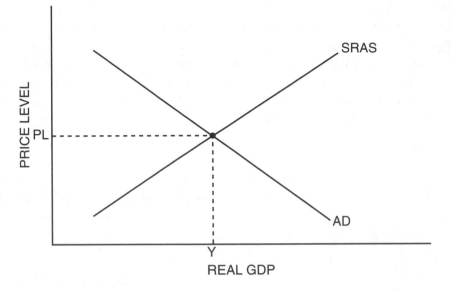

4. How will firms' unit cost of production change when there is an increase in government regulation? (*Hint:* compliance with regulations creates a cost for firms.) Use the following AS/AD diagram to show how an increase in regulations on firms affects SRAS, real GDP, and the price level.

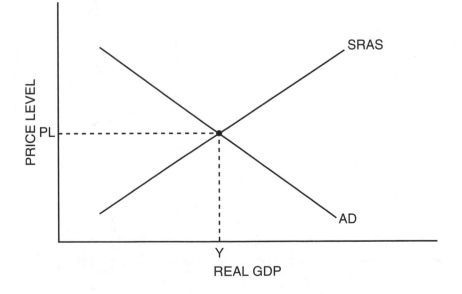

Assume that the economy suffers a negative supply shock and that input prices are completely flexible. In the absence of any fiscal or monetary policy, explain how the economy will return to full employment. To help you reach the correct conclusion, answer the following questions.

5. Immediately following the supply shock, what happens to unemployment?

6. How will high unemployment in the economy affect both product prices and wages if prices and wages are completely flexible?

7. How do firms respond to a decrease in input prices?

8. What effect will firms' response to the decrease in input prices have on SRAS?

Monetary and Fiscal Policy Interactions

In the figures accompanying each question, illustrate the short-run effects for each monetary and fiscal policy combination using the money market, the loanable funds market, and aggregate supply/aggregate demand (AS/AD) graph. Circle the up or down arrow (or ? for uncertain), and explain the effect of the policies on real gross domestic product (GDP), the price level, unemployment, interest rates, and investment.

1. The unemployment rate is 10 percent, and the inflation rate is 2 percent. The federal government cuts personal income taxes and increases its spending. The Federal Reserve (the Fed) buys bonds on the open market.

Figure 5-5.1
Expansionary Monetary and Fiscal Policy

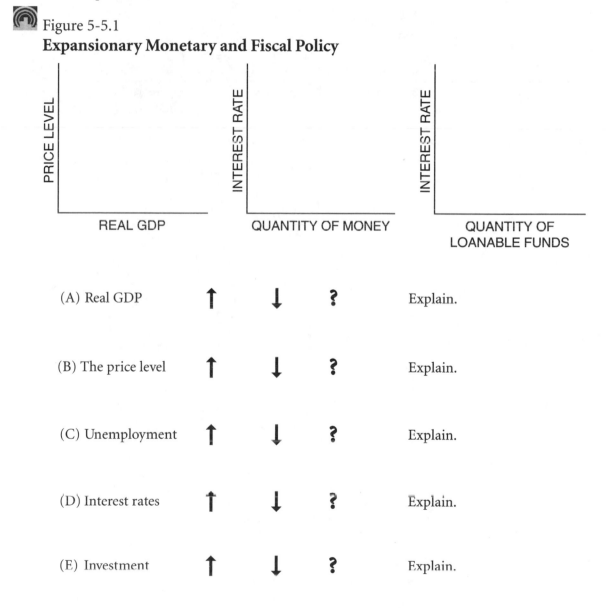

(A) Real GDP	↑	↓	?	Explain.
(B) The price level	↑	↓	?	Explain.
(C) Unemployment	↑	↓	?	Explain.
(D) Interest rates	↑	↓	?	Explain.
(E) Investment	↑	↓	?	Explain.

2. The unemployment rate is 6 percent, and the inflation rate is 9 percent. The federal government raises personal income taxes and cuts spending. The Fed sells bonds on the open market.

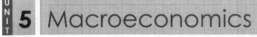

Figure 5-5.2
Contractionary Monetary and Fiscal Policy

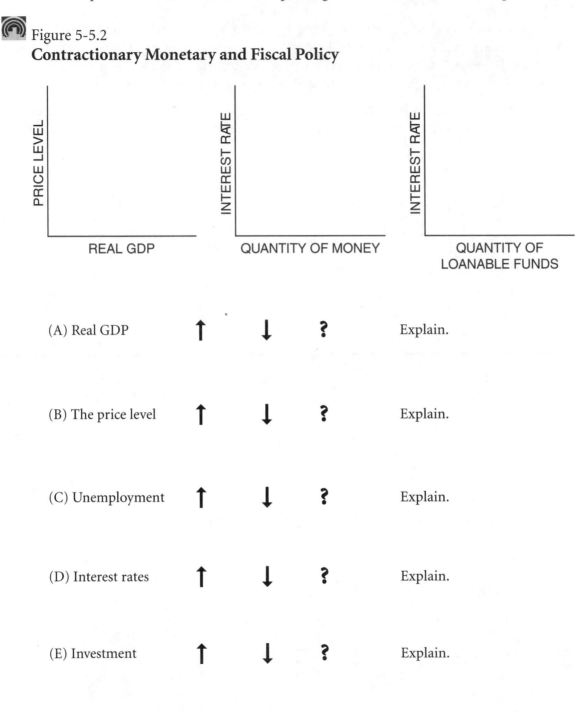

(A) Real GDP	↑	↓	?	Explain.
(B) The price level	↑	↓	?	Explain.
(C) Unemployment	↑	↓	?	Explain.
(D) Interest rates	↑	↓	?	Explain.
(E) Investment	↑	↓	?	Explain.

3. The unemployment rate is 6 percent, and the inflation rate is 5 percent. The federal government cuts personal income taxes and maintains current spending. The Fed sells bonds on the open market.

Figure 5-5.3
Contractionary Monetary Policy and Expansionary Fiscal Policy

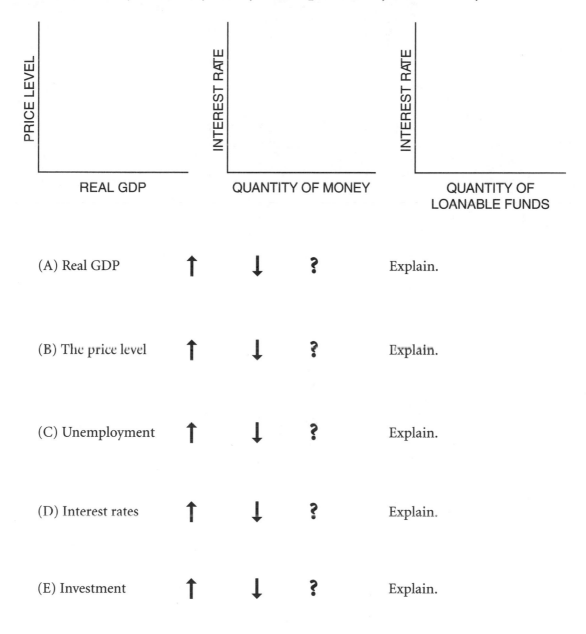

(A) Real GDP   ↑   ↓   ?   Explain.

(B) The price level   ↑   ↓   ?   Explain.

(C) Unemployment   ↑   ↓   ?   Explain.

(D) Interest rates   ↑   ↓   ?   Explain.

(E) Investment   ↑   ↓   ?   Explain.

The Deficit and the Debt

The two primary tools of discretionary fiscal policy are government spending (G) and taxes (T). When government conducts expansionary fiscal policy to counteract recession, G increases and/ or T decreases. When G increases and/or T decreases, the government budget moves toward deficit. A budget deficit occurs when the government spends more than it collects in taxes and borrows to cover the difference. It does this by issuing bonds. The sum of past deficits is the debt. The debt incurs annual interest charges.

When the government conducts contractionary fiscal policy to alleviate inflationary pressures, G decreases and/or T increases. When G decreases and/or T increases, the government budget moves toward surplus. A budget surplus happens when the government taxes more than it spends. The surplus can be used to reduce the debt.

The effect of government borrowing can be modeled using the loanable funds market. A government budget deficit results in an increase in the demand (D) for loanable funds. A budget surplus reduces the demand for loanable funds. It results in an increase in the supply (S) of loanable funds if government pays off the debt.

1. Complete Table 5-6.1. Circle deficit or surplus, and in the other columns place an up arrow for increase, a down arrow for decrease, or NC for no change.

Table 5-6.1
Budget Effects of Fiscal Policy

Fiscal policy	Tools of fiscal policy	Effect on government's budget	Effect on debt	Effect on loanable funds market	Effect on real interest rate
Expansionary	G__ T__	Deficit / Surplus		D__ S__	
Contractionary	G__ T__	Deficit / Surplus		D__ S__	

The central bank of a country can counteract the effect of budget deficits on the real interest rate by conducting an open market purchase of government securities. When the central bank purchases the securities directly from the government, this is referred to as monetizing the debt and is seen as highly inflationary. The effect of an open-market purchase of government securities can be modeled using the money market.

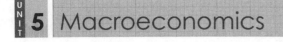

2. Draw a graph of the money market showing how an open-market purchase of government securities affects the nominal interest rate.

3. How would the change in the nominal interest rate affect the real interest rate? Explain.

4. Why is monetizing the debt inflationary?

Crowding Out

Expansionary fiscal policy increases aggregate demand and moves the budget toward deficit. If deficit spending is financed through borrowing, the government will demand loanable funds. The government's demand for loanable funds (D_{lf}) added to the demand for loanable funds by private borrowers. Thus expansionary fiscal policy increases D_{lf} and may cause interest rates to rise. Because the government is borrowing money to finance its expansionary fiscal policy, consumers and businesses will be "crowded out" of financial markets. If consumers and businesses are not able to borrow to finance spending, it will lead to a decrease in aggregate demand (AD).

Crowding out occurs when the government borrows to pursue expansionary fiscal policy and such government borrowing replaces private borrowing and spending. Because some private borrowing and spending is "crowded out" of the economy, part of the increase in aggregate demand from increased government spending (and/or decreased taxes) is offset by a decrease in aggregate demand from decreased consumption and investment as interest rates rise.

Figure 5-7.1
Crowding Out

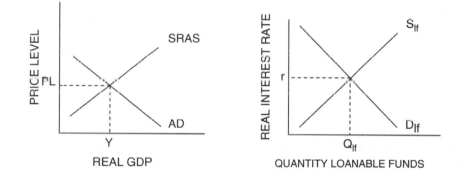

1. Assume fiscal policy is expansionary and the government funds the resulting deficit through borrowing. In Figure 5-7.1, shift one curve in each graph to illustrate the effect of the fiscal policy, and label the new equilibrium values.

2. How will the change in the equilibrium interest rate in the loanable funds market affect the short-run aggregate supply (SRAS) curve in the long run? Show on the AS/AD graph above, and explain.

Short-Run Phillips Curve

The Phillips curve relationship was first proposed by A. W. Phillips in 1958. Following up on Phillips's research, other economists found an inverse relationship between the inflation rate and the unemployment rate. In other words, when inflation increased, the unemployment rate decreased, and when inflation decreased, the unemployment rate increased. A graphic representation of this trade-off became known as the *Phillips curve*.

Student Alert: **Pay close attention to the axes when you graph Phillips curves!**

Figure 5-8.1 shows a Phillips curve. The curve illustrates the trade-off between inflation and unemployment.

Figure 5-8.1
Phillips Curve

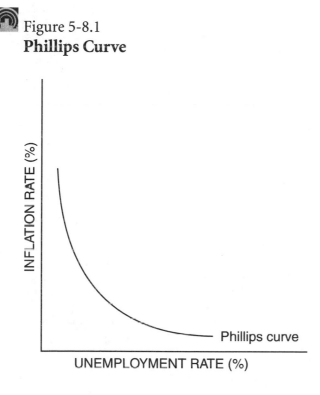

Data from the 1960s appeared to support the Phillips curve relationship. When inflation was low, the unemployment rate was high. The Phillips curve suggested that when the unemployment rate is higher than the natural rate of unemployment and the economy is not operating at its potential gross domestic product (GDP), decreasing unemployment would lead to higher inflation.

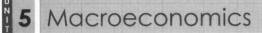

1. Assume that the economy begins in short-run equilibrium as shown in Figure 5-8.2. Graph the effect on the equilibrium price level (PL) and real GDP (Y) if there is a decrease in aggregate demand (AD). Label the equilibrium price level and real GDP after the decrease in aggregate demand as PL$_2$ and Y$_2$.

Figure 5-8.2
Aggregate Demand Decrease

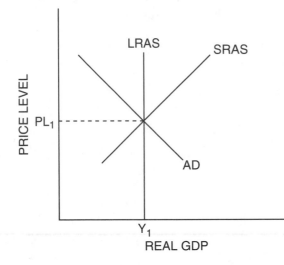

2. What happens to each of the following in the short run?

Real GDP _____   The unemployment rate _____

The price level _____   Real wages _____

3. Draw a graph of a short-run Phillips curve on the following page. Make sure you label your axes correctly. You will plot PL$_1$ and PL$_2$ along with their corresponding unemployment rates. There are no numbers for PL$_1$ and PL$_2$, just plot PL$_1$ at some level and then plot PL$_2$ either above or below it, as shown in the graph above. Then select some unemployment rate (U$_1$) to go with PL$_1$ and then plot U$_2$ either above or below U$_1$ as shown on the graph above. Since the short-run Phillips curve shows the relationship between the inflation rate and the unemployment rate and the aggregate demand/aggregate supply (AD/AS) graph shows the relationship between the price level and real GDP, you need to determine how the change in aggregate demand affects the unemployment rate when the output level changes. Remember that when the economy is in long-run equilibrium, it is at full employment (the unemployment rate is low), and as real GDP falls, the decrease in production causes employment to decrease the unemployment rate to increase.

When the economy of the 1970s experienced high inflation and high unemployment at the same time (i.e., stagflation) the Phillips curve relationship no longer appeared to be true. Eventually, additional data showed that the negative relationship between the inflation rate and the unemployment rate still held, but that the short-run Phillips curve had shifted to the right, as shown in Figure 5-8.3. The rightward shift of the short-run Phillips curve was due to a negative supply shock—a decrease in aggregate supply caused by an increase the price of oil. A positive supply shock (e.g., an advance in technology) will shift the short-run Phillips curve to the left. A negative (positive) supply shock means that for every given unemployment rate, the corresponding inflation rate is higher (lower).

Figure 5-8.3
Short-Run Phillips Curves

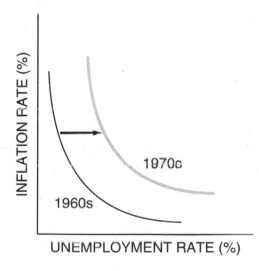

4. Assume the economy begins at long-run equilibrium as shown in Figure 5-8.4. Draw a new
   SRAS curve illustrating the effect of an increase in oil prices. Label the new curve $SRAS_1$, the new
   equilibrium price level PL_3, and the new level of real GDP Y_2.

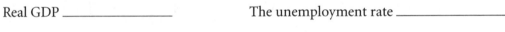

Figure 5-8.4
Effect of an Increase in Oil Prices

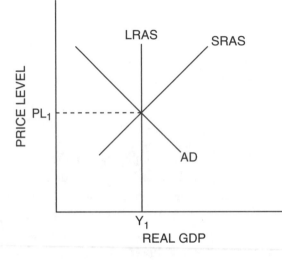

5. Based on your graph, what happens to each of the following in the short run?

   Real GDP _____   The unemployment rate _____

   The price level _____   Real wages _____

6. On the short-run Phillips curve you drew before, plot the inflation and unemployment rates that
   result when the price of oil increases. Remember that a decrease in real GDP means there has been
   a decrease in production, and therefore employment will fall and the unemployment rate will
   increase. This point lies on as SRAS curve that has shifted to the right as a result of the higher oil
   prices.

   Supply shocks are not the only thing that will shift the short-run Phillips curve. The expected rate of
inflation will also cause the short-run Phillips curve to shift. When workers expect inflation they bargain for
higher wage rates, and employers are more willing to grant higher wage rates when they expect to sell their
product for higher prices in the future. When the expected rate of inflation is higher, the short-run Phillips
curve shifts to the right, and the actual rate of inflation increases. If the expected rate of inflation decreases,
the short-run Phillips curve will shift to the left and the actual inflation rate will decrease. Expectations for
inflation lead to change in actual inflation—like a self-fulfilling prophecy.

The Long-Run Phillips Curve and the Role of Expectations

Expectation and the Short-Run Phillips Curve

The short-run Phillips curve (SRPC) is drawn for a given expected rate of inflation and a specific natural rate of unemployment. Changes in inflationary expectations will shift the SRPC. People base their inflationary expectations on information and personal experience, which can result in gaps between the expected rate of inflation and the actual rate of inflation.

1. Suppose the economy is experiencing 2 percent inflation. News of rising energy costs increases people's expectations of inflation. Graph the change in the SRPC.

2. If the government increases spending, how does it affect inflationary expectations? Explain.

3. If people are confident that a new Federal Reserve policy will achieve and maintain price stability, how does it affect inflationary expectations? Explain.

4. What will happen to the actual rate of inflation if people expect a higher inflation rate in the future? What will happen to the actual rate of inflation if people expect a lower inflation rate in the future? Explain.

The Long-Run Phillips Curve

The long-run Phillips curve (LRPC) represents the relationship between unemployment and inflation after the economy has adjusted to inflationary expectations. The LRPC corresponds to the long-run aggregate supply (LRAS) and occurs at the nonaccelerating inflation rate of unemployment (NAIRU). The NAIRU is the unemployment rate at which the unemployment rate does not change over time. The NAIRU corresponds to the full employment level of output and the natural rate of unemployment. Trying to keep the unemployment rate below the NAIRU leads to accelerating inflation rates and cannot be maintained in the long run. Unemployment rates above NAIRU will lead to accelerating deflation that cannot be maintained.

The LRPC is vertical because any unemployment rate above or below the NAIRU cannot be maintained. This means that there is no long-run trade-off between inflation and unemployment—that is, no policy can maintain unemployment rates below the NAIRU in the long run.

5. Draw a graph of the LRPC. Be sure to correctly label the axes and label the point at which the LRPC intersects the horizontal axis.

6. What does the slope of the LRPC indicate about the trade-off between the inflation rate and the unemployment rate?

7. Use the graph in problem 5 to show the effect on the LRPC if the natural rate of unemployment decreases. What happens to the LRAS when the natural rate of unemployment decreases?

Figure 5-9.1
Long-Run Adjustment

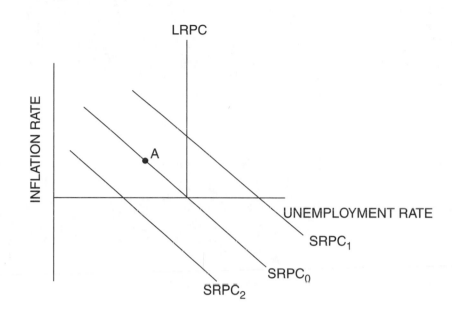

8. What change in inflationary expectations is shown by the shift in the short-run Phillips curve (SRPC) from $SRPC_0$ to $SRPC_1$ in Figure 5-9.1?

9. The LRPC is vertical at the unemployment rate that corresponds to an inflation rate equal to zero. What is the name for this rate of unemployment?

10. At point A on the graph, the actual rate of inflation is (*greater than / less than*) the expected rate of inflation, which will cause the SRPC to shift to the (*right / left*). Label point B on the graph where the economy will be in long-run equilibrium after the change in inflationary expectations. Label point C on the graph where the economy will be if policy makers attempt to keep the unemployment rate where it was at point A after the change in inflationary expectations.

Circle the letter of each correct answer.

1. Which of the following monetary and fiscal policy combinations would definitely cause a decrease in aggregate demand in the short run?

	Discount rate	Government spending	Open market operations
(A)	Decrease	Decrease	Buy bonds
(B)	Decrease	Increase	Buy bonds
(C)	Decrease	Increase	Sell bonds
(D)	Increase	Decrease	Sell bonds
(E)	Increase	Decrease	Buy bonds

2. Which of the following monetary and fiscal policy combinations would definitely cause an increase in aggregate demand?

	Reserve requirements	Taxes	Government spending
(A)	Decrease	Decrease	Decrease
(B)	Decrease	Decrease	Increase
(C)	Increase	Decrease	Increase
(D)	Increase	Increase	Decrease
(E)	Increase	Decrease	Decrease

3. Assume that the economy has a low unemployment rate and a high rate of inflation. Which of the following sets of monetary and fiscal policies would be consistent and designed to reduce the rate of inflation?

	Discount rate	Government spending	Open market operations
(A)	Increase	Increase	Buys bonds
(B)	Increase	Increase	Sell bonds
(C)	Increase	Decrease	Sell bonds
(D)	Increase	Decrease	Buy bonds
(E)	Decrease	Decrease	Buy bonds

4. To counter the crowding-out effect on interest rates caused by the government's deficit spending, the Federal Reserve can

(A) cut tax rates.

(B) increase tax rates.

(C) increase the discount rate.

(D) increase the reserve requirement.

(E) buy bonds through open market operations.

5. Which of the following is a supply-side policy designed to increase real GDP?

(A) A tax credit on capital investment

(B) An increase in business taxes

(C) An increase in government regulation

(D) An increase in government spending

(E) A reduction in the reserve requirement

6. How do the effects of an increase in SRAS compare to the effects of an increase in aggregate demand? An increase in SRAS will increase

(A) real GDP, while the increase in AD will not.

(B) both real GDP and the price level, while the increase in AD will only increase real GDP.

(C) neither real GDP nor the price level, which is the same effect as the increase in AD.

(D) real GDP but not the price level, while the increase in AD will increase both real GDP and the price level.

(E) only the price level, while the increase in AD will increase only real GDP.

7. An expansionary fiscal policy will result in an increase in the interest rate unless which of the following occurs?

   (A) Taxes are cut instead of government expenditures being increased.

   (B) The money supply is increased.

   (C) Wage and price controls are imposed.

   (D) The exchange rate is fixed.

   (E) The Federal Reserve sells government bonds.

8. An expansionary monetary policy may promote long-run growth if it leads to

   (A) an increase in consumption.

   (B) an increase in investment.

   (C) an increase in government spending.

   (D) a constant level of government spending.

   (E) a decrease in net exports.

9. If the government increases spending without a tax increase and simultaneously no monetary-policy changes are made, which of the following would most likely occur?

   (A) Income would not rise at all because no new money is available for increased consumer spending.

   (B) The rise in income may be greater than the multiplier would predict because the higher interest rates will stimulate investment spending.

   (C) The rise in income may be smaller than the multiplier would predict because the higher interest rates will crowd out private investment spending.

   (D) Income will go up by exactly the amount of the new government spending since this acts as a direct injection to the income stream.

   (E) Income will not go up unless taxes are cut as well.

10. Which of the following best describes the chain of events known as "crowding out" as a result of expansionary fiscal policy resulting in a budget deficit?

	Demand for LF	Interest rates	Investment
(A)	Increase	Increase	Increase
(B)	Increase	Increase	Decrease
(C)	Increase	Decrease	Increase
(D)	Decrease	Increase	Increase
(E)	Decrease	Decrease	Decrease

11. In order to be called an automatic, or built-in, stabilizer, which of the following must taxes automatically do in a recessionary period and in an inflationary period?

	Recessionary period	Inflationary period
(A)	Decrease	Decrease
(B)	Decrease	Increase
(C)	Increase	Decrease
(D)	Increase	Increase
(E)	No change	No change

12. When the unemployment rate is 10 percent and the CPI is rising at 2 percent, the federal government cuts taxes and increases government spending. If the Federal Reserve buys bonds on the open market, interest rates, investment, real gross domestic product (GDP), and the price level are most likely to change in which of the following ways?

	Interest rates	Investment	Real GDP	Price level
(A)	Decrease	Decrease	Increase	Increase
(B)	Decrease	Increase	Increase	Increase
(C)	Increase	Decrease	Decrease	Decrease
(D)	Increase	Decrease	Increase	Increase
(E)	Increase	Increase	Increase	Increase

13. When the unemployment rate is 4.5 percent and the CPI is rising at a 12 percent rate, the federal government raises taxes and cuts government spending. If the Federal Reserve sells bonds on the open market, interest rates, investment, real gross domestic product (GDP), and the price level are most likely to change in which of the following ways?

	Interest rates	Investment	Real GDP	Price level
(A)	Decrease	Decrease	Increase	Increase
(B)	Increase	Decrease	Increase	Increase
(C)	Increase	Decrease	Decrease	Decrease
(D)	Decrease	Increase	Increase	Increase
(E)	Decrease	Decrease	Increase	Increase

14. The statement that "the cost of reducing the rate of inflation is that people must lose their jobs" indicates that the speaker believes in a relationship that is usually depicted by which of the following?

    (A) The short-run Phillips curve
    (B) The liquidity trap
    (C) The production function
    (D) The quantity theory of money
    (E) The spending multiplier

15. In the short run, combining an expansionary fiscal policy with a tight money policy is most likely to cause

    (A) real GDP to increase.
    (B) real GDP to decrease.
    (C) interest rates to fall.
    (D) interest rates to rise.
    (E) the federal budget deficit to decrease.

16. Automatic stabilizers in the economy include which of the following?

    I. A progressive personal income tax
    II. Unemployment compensation
    III. Congressional action that increases tax rates

    (A) I only
    (B) II only
    (C) III only
    (D) I and II only
    (E) I and III only

17. Which of the following will move the government budget toward surplus?

    (A) Expansionary fiscal policy
    (B) Contractionary fiscal policy
    (C) Contractionary monetary policy
    (D) A recession
    (E) Supply-side growth policies

18. Which of the following is true about the relationship between the deficit and the debt? They

    (A) are inversely related.
    (B) are equal in most years.
    (C) both increase every year in the United States.
    (D) are positively related.
    (E) must both be paid off at regular intervals.

19. The Phillips curve shows the relationship between

    (A) unemployment and economic growth.
    (B) unemployment and full employment.
    (C) inflation and unemployment.
    (D) inflation and investment.
    (E) inflation and real interest rates.

20. Which of the following is true for the long-run Phillips curve? It

(A) is horizontal.

(B) shows no relationship between the inflation rate and the unemployment rate.

(C) shows the point where the expected rate of inflation exceeds the actual rate of inflation.

(D) is negatively sloped.

(E) does not change if the natural rate of unemployment changes.

MACROECONOMICS

Economic Growth and Productivity

Unit 6

- Economic growth is measured by changes in real gross domestic product or by changes in real GDP per capita.

- Long-run economic growth can be illustrated using a production possibilities curve or a long-run aggregate supply curve. It is shown graphically as a rightward shift of a nation's long-run aggregate supply curve or a rightward shift of its production possibilities curve.

- Long-run economic growth is concerned with increasing an economy's total productive capacity at full employment, also known as its natural rate of output. This output is represented by a vertical long-run aggregate supply curve.

- The rate of economic growth depends largely on increasing productivity. Productivity is affected by a variety of factors including investment in physical capital, increases in human capital, and technological progress.

- Governments can promote economic growth by promoting productivity growth, including:

  ❑ Investing in physical capital (e.g., providing *infrastructure*— roads, bridges, power lines, information networks)

  ❑ Providing for the development of human capital (e.g., education and training)

  ❑ Facilitating technological progress (e.g., research and development)

  ❑ Providing political stability, enforcing property rights, and providing the optimal amount of government intervention.

Economic Growth

Long-Run Aggregate Supply and the Production Possibilities Curve

The long-run aggregate supply (LRAS) curve is vertical at the full-employment level of output. This means that LRAS doesn't change as the price level changes. The location of the LRAS depends on the productive capacity of the economy. Developing more/better resources or improving technology will shift the LRAS curve outward.

The LRAS curve represents a point on an economy's production possibilities curve (PPC). Remember that the PPC represents the maximum output that can be produced given scarce resources. The economy grows if the PPC shifts outward because of more/better resources or technological advances. For the same reason, the LRAS curve shifts outward with more/better resources or if there are technological advances.

Aggregate output in the economy can actually be greater than LRAS in the short run. This means that resources are being used more intensively. For example, workers can work double hours in the short run. However, they can't continue to work that number of hours in the long run. Eventually, the equilibrium level of output will always return to the full-employment level. Aggregate output can only increase in the long run if the LRAS has increased.

Student Alert: Make sure you don't confuse real gross domestic product (GDP) changes in the short run due to business cycles with long-run economic growth!

Use the graphs in Figure 6-1.1 to answer the questions that follow.

Figure 6-1.1

Aggregate Supply and Production Possibilities Curves

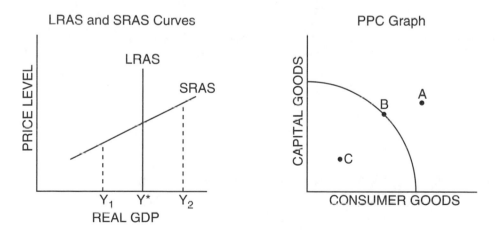

1. What does a PPC show? What are the assumptions about resources and technology in the PPC model?

The maximum output that can be produced given scarce resources. Resources and technology help shift the PPC outward.

2. List two things that could happen to allow the economy to produce at Point A.

3. In Figure 6-1.1, Y^*, Y_1, and Y_2 in the aggregate supply graph correspond to which points on the PPC graph? Explain.

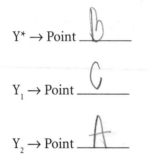

$Y^* \rightarrow$ Point _B_

$Y_1 \rightarrow$ Point _C_

$Y_2 \rightarrow$ Point _A_

4. List two things that could happen to allow the economy to produce Y_2 output.

5. How can the economy produce at Y_2 in the short run? If it is producing at Y_2 in the short run, what will happen in the long run? Explain.

Productivity

Economic Growth and the Determinants of Productivity

An economy's productive capacity is determined by the quantity/quality of its productive resources and technology. In the short run an economy's total productive capacity is fixed, but in the long run an economy can increase its capacity to produce goods and services by increasing the quantity and/or the quality of its productive resources or through technological progress.

An economy's productive capacity is determined by the quantity and quality of its resources, including:

- **Human resources:** labor resources and *human capital*. Human capital refers to the education and skills possessed by labor resources. Education is an investment in human capital because it increases workers' ability to produce.

- **Natural resources:** the gifts of nature that are useful in producing goods and services.

- **Capital goods:** goods (e.g., equipment and machinery) used to make other goods and services.

- **Technology:** technology refers to the way that resources are combined to produce goods and services. Technological progress means that there is a new and better way to produce. Technological progress occurs when production becomes more efficient—that is, when more output can be produced using the same inputs.

Economic growth is often measured by changes in real gross domestic product (GDP) or real GDP per capita. For example, the rate of economic growth can be measured by the average annual percentage change in real GDP per capita. Real GDP per capita is often used to measure living standards across time and between countries. Economic growth occurs because an economy experiences technical progress, increased investments in physical capital, and increased investments in human capital. In the most fundamental sense, economic growth is concerned with increasing an economy's total productive capacity at full employment.

Measuring Economic Growth in Hamilton County and Jefferson County

1. Use Table 6-2.1 to fill out Tables 6-2.2, 6-2.3, and 6-2.4. Recall that a percentage change is equal to the change divided by the starting value.

 Table 6-2.1

Year	Hamilton real GDP	Hamilton population	Jefferson real GDP	Jefferson population
1	$2.1 billion	70,000	$500,000	15
2	$2.5 billion	80,000	$525,000	16
3	$2.8 billion	90,000	$600,000	17
4	$2.7 billion	86,000	$650,000	18

 Table 6-2.2

Time period	Hamilton % change in real GDP	Jefferson % change in real GDP
From Year 1 to Year 2		
From Year 2 to Year 3		
From Year 3 to Year 4		

Table 6-2.3

Year	Hamilton per capita real GDP	Jefferson per capita real GDP
1		
2		
3		
4		

Table 6-2.4

Time period	Hamilton % change in per capita real GDP	Jefferson % change in per capita real GDP
From Year 1 to Year 2		
From Year 2 to Year 3		
From Year 3 to Year 4		

Advanced Placement Economics Macroeconomics: Student Resource Manual © Council for Economic Education, New York, N.Y.

2. When did Hamilton County experience the largest growth in real GDP? _____

   (A) When did Hamilton County experience the largest growth in per capita real GDP? _____

   (B) Why are these growth rates different?

3. When did Jefferson County experience the largest growth in real GDP? _____

   (A) When did Jefferson County experience the largest growth in per capita real GDP? _____

   (B) Why are these growth rates different?

4. Which county do you believe is better off? Explain.

Analyzing Economic Growth

5. Economic growth can be illustrated using both the LRAS curve and the PPC. Use the following graphs to illustrate economic growth.

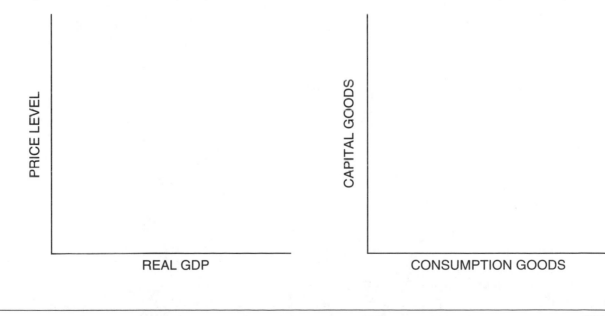

Policies to Promote Economic Growth

A country experiences economic growth if it has increased its long-run ability to produce goods and services, no matter the current short-run phase of the nation's business cycle. Recall that short-run fluctuations in the business cycle are caused by changes in either aggregate demand or short-run aggregate supply. These short-run changes lead to increases, or decreases, in real gross domestic product (GDP). However, these changes are movements around the long-run stability of full-employment GDP. So another way to think about economic growth is to consider the level of real GDP when the nation is at full employment. If this level of full-employment output, as seen by the location of the long-run aggregate supply curve in Figure 6-3.1, is increasing, the nation is experiencing real growth.

Using the production possibilities model, economic growth is shown as an outward movement of the production possibilities curve, as shown in Figure 6-3.1. This allows a nation to produce combinations of goods and services that were previously unattainable, given the nation's stock of resources and technology.

Figure 6-3.1
Long-Run Economic Growth

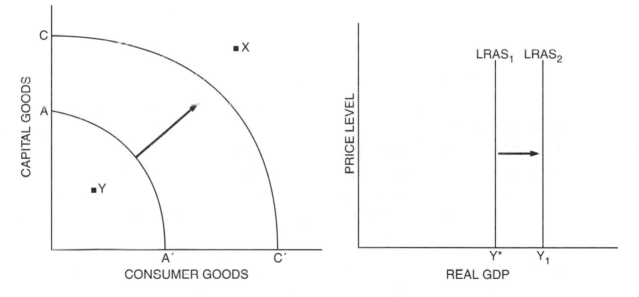

Does each of the following policies lead to economic growth? State yes or no and explain.

1. The government provides subsidies and tax incentives for firms to research new, more efficient, technology in production.

2. With renewed emphasis on education, the nation's high school graduation rate increases from 70 percent to 85 percent, and the literacy rate rises from 98 percent to 99.5 percent.

3. The central bank expands the money supply in an attempt to boost spending and recover from a recession.

4. Because the nation is experiencing unusually low rates of spending and high unemployment, the government lowers household income tax rates and increases military spending.

Government Policies to Promote Long-Run Economic Growth

The key to economic growth is the productivity of the nation where productivity is commonly measured as the quantity of goods and services produced from each unit of labor. The following factors contribute to a nation's productivity, and thus its economic growth.

Capital per worker. A country's workforce is more productive if the workforce has more and better tools with which to work. When tools are produced as physical capital, they are themselves paired with labor to produce goods and services. Therefore, if a country invests in capital production, the country's workforce will be more productive. The thing about capital tools is that they wear out (depreciate) so they must always be replaced at a rate that outpaces the rate of depreciation. The government can promote economic growth through policies that encourage investment in physical capital.

In addition to the private capital workers use to produce goods and services, a country has public capital used for production. This type of capital is known as *infrastructure*. Governments invest directly in physical capital by providing infrastructure such as roads, bridges, power lines, and information networks.

Human capital per worker. In addition to using the physical capital tools, the workforce also uses its collective experience and education to produce goods and services. Human capital can be acquired through formal schooling, occupational training, or simply accumulated experience at the workplace. Human capital, like physical capital, depreciates over time. Governments promote economic growth by investing in the country's human capital, through investment in its education system.

Natural resources per worker. Natural resources are production inputs that come from the world around us. These resources include minerals, sources of energy, rivers, forests, and fisheries. A country's workforce can be more productive when they have abundant natural resources, but to ensure long-run economic growth, the quality of those resources should be protected and they should be sustainably extracted. For example, a country might have a very large supply of clean water or timber, but if that renewable water or timber resource is used at a rate faster than the regeneration rate, the resource will be exhausted. Likewise, all the water in the world won't do a country any good if it's polluted. In other words, natural resources can also be depreciated and rendered unproductive unless the government protects and invests in them.

Technology. A country's state of knowledge is the understanding of how best to produce goods and services. A country with little technology may see the best way to farm a crop is with a mule-drawn plow. A country with better technology can also farm that crop but does it with enormous diesel powered harvesters. The country with better technology can harvest much more output, with the same amount of land, in less time, and at lower per-unit costs. Governments can promote economic growth by facilitating technological progress through research and development.

In addition, governments promote economic growth by providing political stability, enforcing property rights, and providing the optimal amount of government intervention.

5. How will each of the following policies affect economic growth and why?

(A) The government raises taxes on businesses.

(B) The government invests in improvements in the national highway system.

(C) Research and development leads to improvements in technology.

(D) Labor productivity increases as a result of a new education initiative.

(E) Expansionary economic policy leads to lower interest rates.

(F) A country's government is unable to enforce property rights and the country is on the verge of a civil war.

(G) Government agencies establish regulations to maintain natural resources at sustainable levels.

6. Draw an aggregate demand and aggregate supply (AS/AD) graph to show the U.S. economy in long-run equilibrium.

(A) Suppose the U.S. economy experiences increased productivity. Show the short-run impact on your graph.

(B) Now suppose that these increased productivity gains last into the long run and create real economic growth in the United States. Show the long-run impact of this growth on real GDP and the price level in the graph.

Circle the letter of each correct answer.

1. Which of the following would best portray long-run economic growth?

   (A) A leftward shift of the aggregate demand curve

   (B) A rightward shift of the aggregate demand curve

   (C) A leftward shift of the production possibilities curve

   (D) A leftward shift of the long-run aggregate supply curve

   (E) A rightward shift of the long-run aggregate supply curve

2. An increase in which of the following would be most likely to increase long-run economic growth? *Productivity is the key to growth.*

   (A) Taxes

   (B) Interest rates

   (C) Consumer spending

   (D) Productivity

   (E) Value of domestic currency

Use the following graph to answer questions 3 and 4.

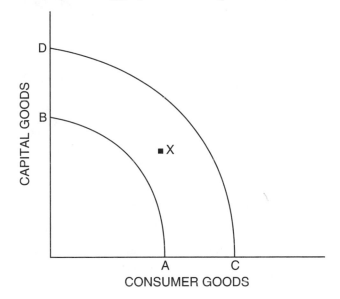

3. If the production possibilities curve of an economy shifts from AB to CD, it most likely is caused by

   (A) full employment of resources.

   (B) technology advances.

   (C) allocative efficiency.

   (D) a decrease in the price level.

   (E) productive efficiency.

4. If the production possibilities curve of an economy is CD and the economy is producing at Point X, which of the following is true?

   (A) Technology advances changed industrial production.

   (B) The quality and quantity of productive resources increased.

   (C) Improvements in productivity led to increased output.

   (D) Resources are not fully employed.

   (E) Aggregate demand decreased.

5. Which of the following is the best measure of economic growth?

(A) Nominal GDP

(B) Real GDP

(C) Nominal GDP per capita

(D) Real GDP per capita

(E) The business cycle

6. Which of the following will cause the PPC to shift outward?

(A) A decrease in unemployment

(B) An increase in aggregate demand

(C) A decrease in the price level

(D) Depreciation of physical capital

(E) Technological change

7. Which of the following is *not* an economic resource?

(A) Physical capital

(B) Human capital

(C) Nature's gifts

(D) Labor

(E) Money

8. Which of the following will lead to an increase in human capital?

(A) Job training

(B) A decrease in wages

(C) An increase in wages

(D) A minimum wage law

(E) Technological change

9. An economy's natural resources include which of the following?

(A) Labor

(B) Entrepreneurship

(C) Population

(D) Technology

(E) Land

10. Which of the following is true of the long-run aggregate supply curve? It

(A) has a positive slope.

(B) is used to determine the phase of the business cycle.

(C) will shift to the left when there is economic growth.

(D) is horizontal at the full-employment level of output.

(E) represents a point on the PPC.

11. The productive capacity of an economy is measured by the

(A) slope of the LRAS curve.

(B) intersection of the SRAS and AD curves.

(C) slope of the PPC.

(D) horizontal intercept of the LRAS. SRASAD intercept

(E) phase of the business cycle.

12. Which of the following is true regarding productivity? It

(A) can be increased by human capital investment in the short run.

(B) is fixed in the short run.

(C) cannot be increased in the long run.

(D) has no effect on an economy's standard of living.

(E) can increase in the long run.

13. Which of the following will not increase productivity?

(A) Investment in human capital

(B) Increases in physical capital

(C) Depreciation of capital stock

(D) Technological change

(E) Increases in the labor force

14. Aggregate output must be
    (A) greater than LRAS.
    (B) less than LRAS.
    (C) equal to LRAS.
    (D) either less than or equal to LRAS.
    (E) increasing if there is economic growth in the economy.

15. Which of the following is a government policy to promote growth?
    (A) Decreasing taxes
    (B) Raising government spending
    (C) Increasing interest rates
    (D) Providing public education
    (E) Regulating businesses

16. Economic growth occurs when
    (A) the economy recovers from a recession.
    (B) monetary policy is effective.
    (C) fiscal policy increases aggregate demand.
    (D) the economy's productive capacity increases.
    (E) nominal GDP increases over time.

17. Which of the following is an example of ~~not~~ infrastructure?
    (A) Roads
    (B) Bridges
    (C) Airports
    (D) Education
    (E) Schools

18. Which of the following is not true of the LRAS curve? It
    (A) is vertical.
    (B) is a function of the price level.
    (C) measures productive capacity.
    (D) represents a point on the PPC.
    (E) shifts as a result of productivity increases.

19. Natural resources are
    (A) always renewable.
    (B) never renewable.
    (C) not important for long-run economic growth.
    (D) subject to depreciation.
    (E) part of physical capital.

20. Governments can promote economic growth by providing which of the following?
    (A) Excessive government intervention
    (B) High tax rates
    (C) Political stability
    (D) Common property
    (E) Private investment

(handwritten notes) lower rr rate decrease discount rate ↓ federal funds rate

C → A = Expansionary Monetary; buy bonds
Fiscal: cut taxes increase gov spend

C = Recession
A = Full employment
B = Unattainable
Desired.

A → B: improvement in technology → more productivity

(handwritten graph: Capital Goods vs Consumer Goods with points A, B, C)

LR economic monetary: make intrest rates ↓
fiscal: ↑ crowding intrts out effect.

MACROECONOMICS

Open Economy: International Trade and Finance

Finance

Unit 7

- A country's balance of payments accounts are a summary of all of the country's transactions with other countries.

- There are two important accounts within the balance of payments: the *current account* and the *financial account* (formerly known as the *capital account*). The current account records a country's exports and imports of goods and services, net investment income, and net transfers. The financial account records the difference between a country's sale of assets to foreigners and its purchase of assets from foreigners.

- The current account includes the country's trade balance (net exports).

- The financial account measures capital inflows in the form of foreign savings that finance domestic investment and government borrowing.

- The current account and the financial account must sum to zero.

- Capital flows between countries occur when the loanable funds markets in the two countries establish different equilibrium real interest rates. Financial capital will flow into the country where the real interest rate is higher.

- Trade barriers such as tariffs and quotas limit the gains from trade. These barriers generally protect domestic sellers at the expense of domestic buyers.

- To trade, nations must exchange currencies.

- An exchange rate is the price of one currency in terms of another. Foreign exchange markets use supply and demand to set exchange rates.

- Appreciation is an increase in the value of a nation's currency in foreign exchange markets. Appreciation of a nation's currency decreases exports and increases imports.

- Depreciation is a decrease in the value of a nation's currency in foreign exchange markets. Depreciation of a nation's currency increases exports and decreases imports.

- Monetary and fiscal policies can affect exchange rates, the international balance of trade, and the balance of payments.

- Domestic economic policies affect international trade, and international trade affects the domestic economy. The international sector influences unemployment, inflation, and economic growth.

Balance of Payments Accounts

A country's *balance of payments* accounts are a summary of all of the country's transactions with other countries. There are two important accounts within the balance of payments: the *current account* and the *financial account* (formerly known as the *capital account*). The current account records a nation's exports and imports of goods and services, and also includes net investment income and net transfers. The financial account records the difference between a country's sale of assets to foreigners and its purchase of assets from foreigners. The balance of payments is essential for making sense of a nation's position in the global economy.

The current account records a nation's exports and imports of goods and services. It also includes net investment income (U.S. earnings on investment abroad *minus* foreign earnings from capital invested in the United States) and net transfers (e.g., foreign aid sent to other countries and funds that immigrants send to family abroad).

The financial account records the flows of money from the purchase and sale of assets domestically and abroad. For example, U.S. investors might buy a hotel building in Tokyo or shares of stock in a Swedish company while foreign investors might buy a factory in the United States or stock in a U.S. company. Foreign assets are bought and sold using currencies purchased on foreign exchange markets. The financial flows recorded in the financial account are part of the loanable funds market. Foreign investors provide funds that are used to purchase assets, which means they supply loanable funds. Changes in the supply of loanable funds affect the equilibrium real interest rate in the loanable funds market, which then affects a country's investment, aggregate demand, output, employment, and price level.

When classifying a transaction, consider whether a country uses (loses) or earns (gains) foreign currency. If the international transaction *uses* foreign currency to complete the transaction, it is a *debit* (*negative*). If it *earns* foreign currency, it is a *credit* (*positive*).

1. Evaluate each of the transactions on the U.S. balance of payments and complete Table 7-2.1.
   Check either debit or credit, and current account or financial account.

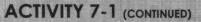 Table 7-1.1

Transactions on the U.S. Balance of Payments

	Credit +	Debit −	Current account	Financial account
1. Harley-Davidson USA purchases $25 million in production machinery from a Japanese company.		✔	✔	
2. André Prenoor, U.S. entrepreneur, invests $50 million to develop a theme park in Malaysia.				
3. A Chinese company sells $1 million worth of berets to the U.S. Army.				
4. BMW pays $1 million to a U.S. shipper for transporting cars from Germany to the United States.				
5. Each month, Ima Grent, who recently arrived in the United States, sends half her paycheck to her sister in Poland.				
6. Bank of America pays $5 million in interest to French depositors.				
7. Senor Ramos from Spain buys a shopping center in Florida.				
8. A Brazilian investor buys five $10,000 U.S. Treasury bonds.				
9. German tourists spend $3 million in the United States; U.S. tourists spend $5 million in Germany.				
10. Brit-Discz, a London record store, spends $10,000 on CDs by the Generic Gurls, a U.S. kiddy-pop group.				
11. Sam Boney, U.S. ice-rink magnate, buys stock in a Chilean ice-rink chain.				

It is important to understand that *the current account balance and the financial account balance must sum to zero.* Consider the example of a country that imports more than it exports and runs a current account deficit. A surplus in the financial account must offset the current account deficit because the net imports must either be paid for or purchased on credit. That is, the foreign currency used to buy the net imports had to come from somewhere. A financial account surplus must exist to supply the needed foreign currency if there is a current account deficit. In other words, *a current account deficit must come from a financial account surplus and vice versa.*

Assume there are only two countries, country A and country B.

2. If Country A is running a current account surplus, what must be true of Country A's financial account? Explain.

3. Draw a graph of the loanable funds market in Country B and show how an increase in Country A's current account surplus affects the supply of loanable funds and the equilibrium interest rate. Make sure you label all axes and curves.

Barriers to Trade

There are gains from trade. Total output is greater when countries specialize according to their comparative advantage and trade rather than trying to be self-sufficient. The theory of comparative advantage explains the mutual benefits countries receive from free trade. Policies to promote free trade attempt to achieve the efficiency benefits from free trade. For example, groups of countries create free trade areas to promote international trade. Examples of these efforts include the North American Free Trade Agreement (NAFTA), the World Trade Organization (WTO), the European Union (EU), and the Asia-Pacific Economic Cooperation (APEC) Forum.

However, other policies interfere with free trade and prevent countries from receiving the efficiency benefits of free trade. For example, countries sometimes impose trade barriers to protect domestic industries. Trade barriers include tariffs and quotas. A *quota* is a limit on the quantity of imports allowed into a country. A *tariff* is a tax on imports.

In Figure 7-2.1, the demand curve represents the demand by the domestic economy for a commodity that is produced domestically and also imported. The domestic supply curve indicates what the domestic suppliers are willing and able to produce at alternative prices. The total supply includes the domestic supply and the supply of imports. If there were no international trade or a complete ban on imports, the domestic demand and supply would determine the equilibrium price of P and the equilibrium quantity of Q. The total output would be produced by domestic firms.

Figure 7-2.1
International Trade

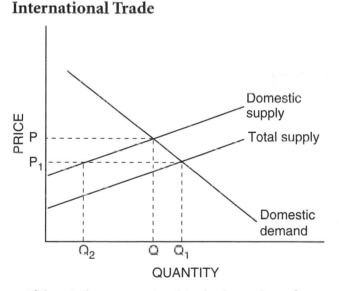

If there is free international trade, the total supply curve represents the production by domestic and foreign producers. Domestic consumers would pay P_1 and consume Q_1. They consume more of the commodity at a lower price. Also, at P_1, domestic firms are producing Q_2 and foreign producers are producing $(Q_1 - Q_2)$. Thus, domestic firms are producing less under free trade than they would if the nation did not import the commodity.

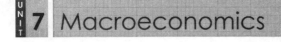

Tariffs

A tariff is a tax on imports. The imposition of a tax increases the cost of each unit, which is represented by a decrease in supply. This would result in an increase in equilibrium price and a decrease in equilibrium quantity.

1. Use Figure 7-2.2 to show the effect of an import tariff of $T per unit. Graph the "Total Supply with Tariff" curve, and indicate the amount of the tariff on the graph. Label the equilibrium price and quantity after the tariff as P_T and Q_T on the graph.

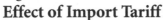 Figure 7-2.2
Effect of Import Tariff

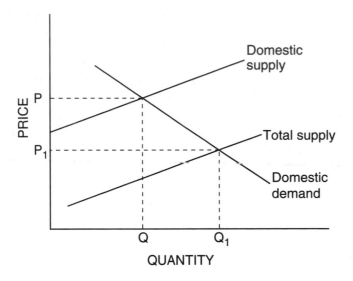

2. What is the effect of the tariff on the equilibrium price and quantity for domestic consumers compared with the free trade levels?

3. Identify the arguments frequently used to impose some type of trade barrier. Discuss the pros and cons of three arguments.

The Foreign Exchange Market

Within an economy prices are stated in the domestic currency. For example, in the United States, prices are stated in dollars and in Europe prices are stated in euros. Buyers use the domestic currency to purchase domestic goods. However, when goods are purchased from another country, they must be paid for in that country's domestic currency. Exporters are paid in the domestic currencies so they can spend it domestically. As a result, international trade requires that currencies also be traded. Currencies are traded in *foreign exchange markets*. The equilibrium price at which currencies are traded is called the *exchange rate*. An exchange rate is the rate at which the currency of one country is exchanged for the currency of another.

Table 7-3.1 shows the exchange rates for selected countries for May and August of the same year.

Table 7-3.1
Exchange Rates

	Cost of foreign currency in U.S. dollars (U.S. dollars/foreign currency)		Cost of U.S. dollar in foreign currency (foreign currency/U.S. dollars)	
	May	August	May	August
British pound	1.4	1.8	0.71	0.56
Canadian dollar	0.64	0.63	1.5625	1.5873
European euro	0.87	0.91	1.149	1.099
Swedish krona	0.094	0.093	10.638	10.753
Japanese yen	0.0083	0.0090	120.482	111.111
Mexican peso	0.1101	0.1502	9.083	6.6558

Use the data in the table to calculate the cost of the following products in U.S. dollars. To solve, divide the cost of the product in the foreign currency by the cost of the U.S. dollar in the foreign currency. Indicate whether the dollar has appreciated or depreciated between May and August.

	May	August	Appreciated or Depreciated
1. A dinner for two that costs 500 Mexican pesos			
2. A hotel room that costs 30,000 Japanese yen			
3. A BMW that costs 85,000 euros in Germany			
4. A pound of Swedish meatballs that costs 30 kronor			
5. A pair of pants that costs 72 pounds in London			
6. A leather jacket that costs 1,800 Canadian dollars			

When Americans buy foreign goods, U.S. dollars are supplied in the foreign exchange market and the foreign currency is demanded. When foreigners buy U.S. goods, the foreign currency is supplied in foreign exchange markets and the U.S. dollar is demanded. A foreign exchange market determines the equilibrium exchange rate (price) and quantity of currency exchanged using the supply and demand curves for a currency.

An increase in the exchange rate for a currency (which can be caused by an increase in demand or a decrease in supply) is called *appreciation* of that currency. When a currency appreciates, it is said to have strengthened. For example, if the exchange rate increases in the market for dollars, it means that it takes more of the foreign currency to purchase a dollar. This means that a dollar can buy more of the foreign currency. A decrease in the exchange rate for a currency (which can be caused by a decrease in demand or an increase in supply) is called *depreciation* of that currency. When a currency depreciates, it is said to have weakened. For example, if the exchange rate decreases in the market for dollars, it means that it takes less of the foreign currency to purchase a dollar. This means it takes more dollars to buy the foreign currency.

Appreciation or depreciation of a currency changes the price of imports and exports. When a country's currency appreciates, it is more expensive for foreigners to buy the country's exports and it is cheaper for the country to buy imports. When a country's currency depreciates, it is cheaper for foreigners to buy the country's exports and it is more expensive for the country to buy imports. Appreciation and depreciation of a currency will affect the economy because they affect net exports.

Consider the following situations. In each case, an underlying event causes a change in foreign exchange markets. Graph the effect on the equilibrium exchange rate and currency exchanged in the foreign exchange markets as shown in the example.

Student Alert: **Pay close attention to correct labeling on foreign exchange market graphs!**

EXAMPLE: The prices of U.S. goods rise relative to the prices of German goods.

Figure 7-3.1
Prices of U.S. Goods Increase

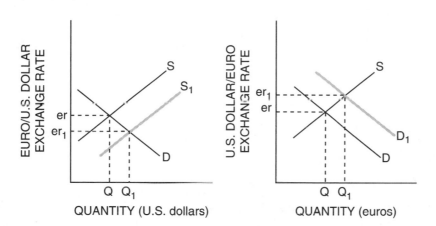

QUANTITY (U.S. dollars)   QUANTITY (euros)

Rationale: *Americans will demand the less expensive German goods. To purchase the German goods, they need euros, so the demand for euros increases (shifts to the right). To buy euros, the Americans will supply U.S. dollars to the foreign exchange market, so the supply of U.S. dollars shifts to the right. The U.S. dollar depreciates (the exchange rate decreases). The euro appreciates (the exchange rate increases).*

7. Real interest rates in the United States rise faster than real interest rates in Canada.

Figure 7-3.2
Real Interest Rates in the United States Increase

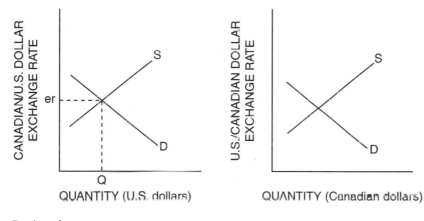
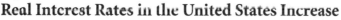

QUANTITY (U.S. dollars)   QUANTITY (Canadian dollars)

Rationale:

8. French tourists flock to Mexico's beaches.

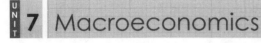Figure 7-3.3
French Tourists Visit Mexico

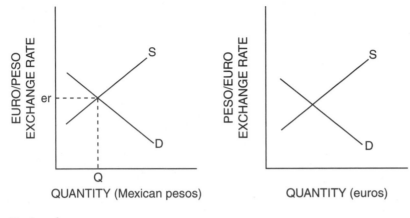

Rationale:

9. Japanese video games become popular with U.S. children.

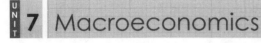Figure 7-3.4
U.S. Children Want Videos Produced in Japan

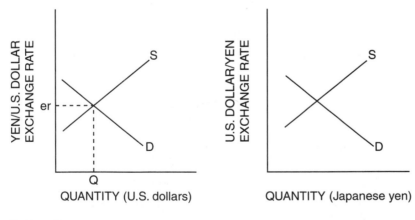

Rationale:

How Monetary and Fiscal Policies Affect Exchange Rates

Changes in a nation's monetary and fiscal policies affect its exchange rates and its balance of trade through the real interest rate, income, and the price level. Changes in the value of a country's currency affect the balance of trade, which affects aggregate demand. Changes in aggregate demand affect real output and the price level. In other words, domestic policies influence currency values, and currency values influence domestic policies. Policy makers cannot ignore the international effects of changes in monetary and fiscal policies.

For each scenario, show the effect on equilibrium interest rate and quantity of currency in the foreign exchange market graphs in Figures 7-4.1 through 7-4.5. Use the graphs to show the starting equilibrium exchange rate and quantity, the shift that occurs, and the new equilibrium exchange rate and quantity. Following each set of graphs, indicate the short-run effect of the change in the foreign exchange market on net exports, aggregate demand, and the price level in the United States.

Figure 7-4.1

Effect on Taiwan If U.S. Government Decreases Taxes

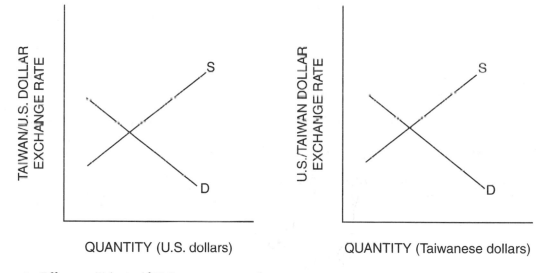

1. Effect on Taiwan if U.S. government decreases taxes:

   (A) U.S. imports (*increase / decrease*). Explain.

   (B) U.S. exports (*increase / decrease*). Explain.

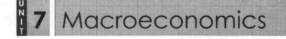
(C) U.S. aggregate demand (*increases / decreases*). Explain.

(D) The price level in the United States (*increases / decreases*). Explain.

Figure 7-4.2
Japan's Real GDP Increases

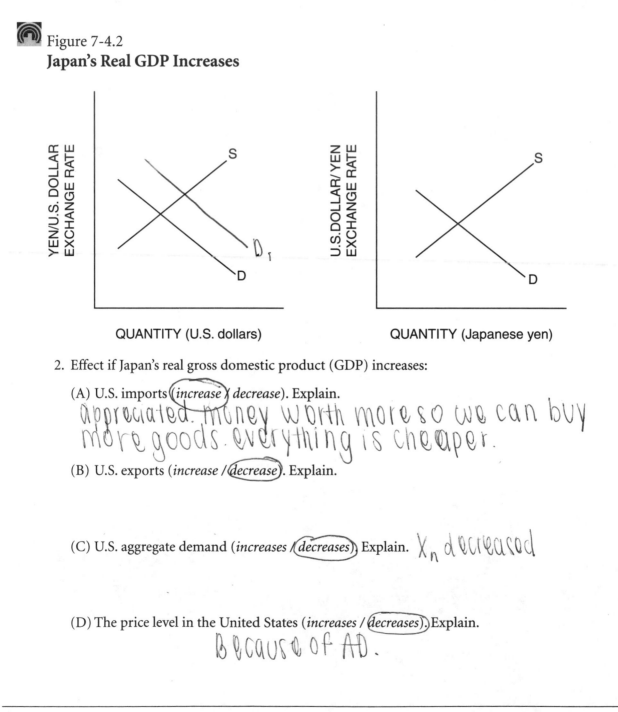

2. Effect if Japan's real gross domestic product (GDP) increases:

(A) U.S. imports (*increase* / *decrease*). Explain.

appreciated. money worth more so we can buy more goods. everything is cheaper.

(B) U.S. exports (*increase* / *decrease*). Explain.

(C) U.S. aggregate demand (*increases* / *decreases*). Explain. X_n decreased

(D) The price level in the United States (*increases* / *decreases*). Explain.
Because of AD.

Figure 7-4.3

Real Interest Rates in the United States Increase Relative to Great Britain

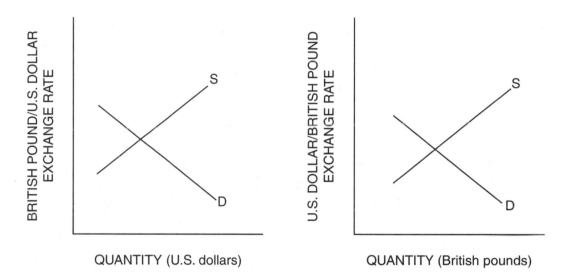

3. Effect if real interest rates in the United States increase relative to Great Britain:

   (A) U.S. imports (*increase* / *decrease*). Explain. demand↑

   appreciated U.S. dollar is more attractive

   (B) U.S. exports (*increase* / *decrease*). Explain.

   The US dollar appreciated.

   (C) U.S. aggregate demand (*increases* / *decreases*). Explain.

   Xn decreased

   (D) The price level in the United States (*increases* / *decreases*). Explain.

   AD shift left

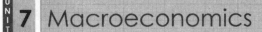

Figure 7-4.4

Europe Experiences a Recession

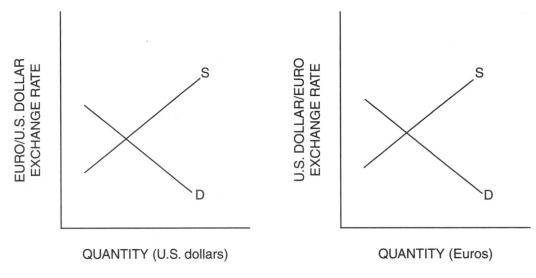

4. Effect if Europe experiences a recession:

(A) U.S. imports (*increase / decrease*). Explain.

(B) U.S. exports (*increase / decrease*). Explain.

(C) U.S. aggregate demand (*increases / decreases*). Explain.

X_n Increase

(D) The price level in the United States (*increases / decreases*). Explain.

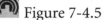
Figure 7-4.5

The Price Level in Canada Increases Relative to the United States

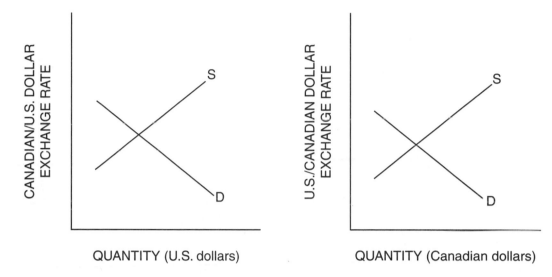

QUANTITY (U.S. dollars)   QUANTITY (Canadian dollars)

5. Effect if the price level in Canada increases relative to the United States:

(A) U.S. imports (*increase / decrease*). Explain.

(B) U.S. exports (*increase / decrease*). Explain.

(C) U.S. aggregate demand (*increases / decreases*). Explain.

(D) The price level in the United States (*increases / decreases*). Explain.

Net Exports and Capital Flows: Linking Financial and Goods Markets

The term *capital flow* refers to the movement of financial capital (money) between economies. *Capital inflows* consist of foreign funds moving into an economy from another country; *capital outflows*, or capital flight, is the opposite—domestic funds moving out of an economy to another country. For example, from the perspective of the U.S. economy, the construction of a new plant by a Japanese automobile manufacturer within the United States is an example of capital inflow. Likewise, when an American manufacturer finances the construction of a plant outside of the United States, it is an example of capital outflow.

The loanable funds market is used to analyze capital flows in an economy. Because financial capital affects the amount of money available for borrowers, changes in capital flows shifts the supply curve for loanable funds.

Capital inflows increase the supply of loanable funds, resulting in the decrease in domestic real interest rates shown in the following graph:

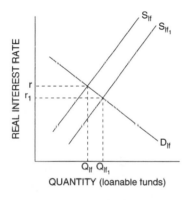

Capital outflows deplete a nation's supply of loanable funds, causing domestic interest rates to increase, as shown in the following graph:

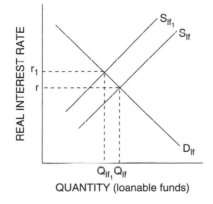

Capital Flows Resulting from a Change in Net Exports

1. Japanese firms have recently increased their imports of American made semiconductors. As a result, the U.S. current account moves toward (*surplus / deficit*) and U.S. net exports will (*increase / decrease*).

2. Illustrate on the graphs provided how the relative exchange rates of the U.S. dollar and Japanese yen will change as a result of the increase in Japanese purchases of U.S. semiconductors. Be sure to label your graphs correctly (e.g., the price of dollars should be stated in terms of yen per dollar, and vice versa).

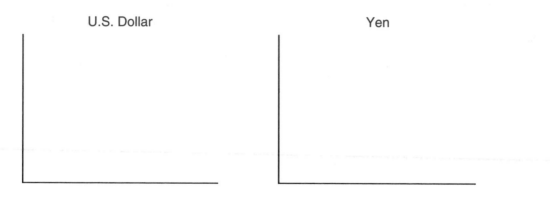

U.S. Dollar   Yen

3. Illustrate on a correctly labeled graph of the loanable funds market in the United States the changes that result from the Japanese importation of U.S. semiconductors. *Hint:* Current account deficits are offset by financial account surpluses (capital inflow) while current account surpluses are offset by financial account deficits (capital outflow).

U.S. Loanable Funds Market

4. Assume that inflation in the United States begins to rise while prices throughout the European Union remain relatively stable. The U.S. current account moves toward (*surplus / deficit*) and U.S. net exports (*increase / decrease*).

5. Illustrate on the graphs provided how the relative exchange rates of the U.S. dollar and euro will change as a result of this change in relative inflation rates. Be sure to label your graphs correctly (e.g., the price of dollars should be stated in terms of euro per dollar, and vice versa).

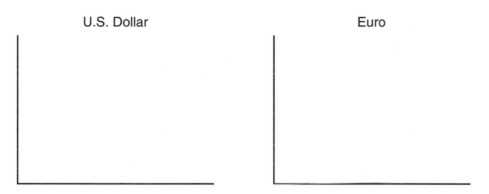

U.S. Dollar   Euro

6. Illustrate on a graph of the loanable funds market in the United States the changes that result when the relative inflation rates change. *Hint:* Current account deficits are offset by financial account surpluses (capital inflow) while current account surpluses are offset by financial account deficits (capital outflow).

U.S. Loanable Funds Market

Capital Flows Resulting from a Change in Policy

7. Due to a recent recession, expansionary fiscal policies in the United States have led to historically large federal budget deficits. On a correctly labeled graph of the loanable funds market in the United States, illustrate the effects of massive government borrowing.

U.S. Loanable Funds Market

8. The recession causes real interest rates to (*increase / decrease*) and foreign investors will (*increase / decrease*) their purchases of bonds in the United States. Illustrate this change on your loanable funds graph above.

9. Assume that the central bank enacts an expansionary policy of purchasing government securities on the open market. This monetary policy will (*increase / decrease*) real interest rates in the United States. As a result of the change in real interest rates, foreign investors will (*increase / decrease*) their purchases of bonds in the United States.

Illustrate this change on a correctly labeled graph of the loanable funds market.

U.S. Loanable Funds Market

Capital Flows Resulting from a Change in Foreign Direct Investment

10. Foreign direct investment (FDI) into the United States rose sharply during the second half of the 1990s due to the perceived strength and stability of the U.S economy relative to unstable economies worldwide. On a correctly labeled graph of the loanable funds market in the United States, illustrate the effect of this influx of FDI.

U.S. Loanable Funds Market

11. Great Britain was a leading investor in American firms at this time. Use correctly labeled graphs of the markets for dollars and pounds to illustrate the relative change in value of these two currencies on the foreign exchange market as a result of British investment in American companies. Be sure to label your graphs correctly (e.g., the price of dollars should be stated in terms of pounds per dollar, and vice versa).

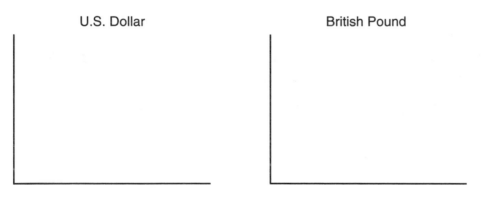

U.S. Dollar   British Pound

12. The changes above will cause U.S. net exports to (*increase* / *decrease*).

13. The U.S. economy slowed in the early 2000s while American firms discovered less costly production possibilities in foreign countries. On a correctly labeled graph of the loanable funds market in the United States, illustrate the effects of this capital flight.

U.S. Loanable Funds Market

Circle the letter of each correct answer.

1. A country's current account includes which of the following?

   (A) Sales of assets to other countries

   (B) Purchases of assets from other countries

   (C) All current automatic payments between countries

   (D) The country's trade balance

   (E) The balance available in the government's Treasury account

2. A country's financial account includes which of the following?

   (A) Net investment income

   (B) Net transfers

   (C) Exports

   (D) Imports

   (E) Sales of assets to other countries

3. What does a balance of trade deficit imply?

   (A) Exports of goods and services exceed imports of goods and services.

   (B) Imports of goods and services exceed exports of goods and services.

   (C) Investment income received from abroad exceeds investment income paid to foreigners.

   (D) Investment income paid to foreigners exceeds investment income received from abroad.

   (E) Investment by foreigners exceeds domestic investment in other countries.

4. If the balance on the current account is zero, which of the following transactions will cause it to go into deficit?

   (A) The Moscow Capital Investment Corporation makes a loan to a U.S. firm.

   (B) A U.S. subsidiary exports raw materials to its French parent company.

   (C) U.S. firms and individuals receive dividends on U.S. investments in Latin America.

   (D) U.S. tourists in Great Britain purchase pounds sterling.

   (E) Foreigners purchase U.S. securities.

5. An increase in U.S. real interest rates relative to the rest of the world can be expected to

   (A) encourage investment spending by U.S. firms in the United States.

   (B) decrease the capital flow into the United States.

   (C) cause a net outflow of foreign capital from the United States.

   (D) increase the international value of the dollar.

   (E) improve the situation for exporters.

6. The current account and the financial account must do which of the following?

   (A) Equal the capital account

   (B) Equal each other

   (C) Move in the same direction

   (D) Equal zero when added together

   (E) Equal 1 when added together

7. Assume a contractionary monetary policy causes real interest rates in the United States to increase relative to Japan. In the short run, the value of the U.S. dollar, the value of the Japanese yen, and the U.S. balance of trade will most likely change in which of the following ways?

	Dollar	Yen	U.S. balance of trade
(A)	Appreciate	Appreciate	Move toward deficit
(B)	Appreciate	Depreciate	Move toward deficit
(C)	Appreciate	Depreciate	Move toward surplus
(D)	Depreciate	Depreciate	Move toward surplus
(E)	No change	Appreciate	Move toward deficit

8. If a nation's currency appreciates, in the short run its net exports and aggregate demand are most likely to change in which of the following ways?

	Net exports	Aggregate demand
(A)	Decrease	Decrease
(B)	Decrease	Increase
(C)	Increase	Decrease
(D)	Increase	Increase
(E)	No change	Decrease

9. If exchange rates are allowed to fluctuate freely and the U.S. demand for Japanese yen increases, which of the following will happen?

(A) The U.S. balance of trade deficit will worsen in the long run.

(B) Americans will have to pay more for Japanese goods.

(C) It will be more expensive for the Japanese to buy American real estate.

(D) The dollar will appreciate.

(E) More Americans will want to travel to Japan.

10. An import tariff will have what effect on price and quantity in the domestic market for the good?

	Price	Quantity
(A)	Increase	Increase
(B)	Increase	Decrease
(C)	Decrease	Increase
(D)	Decrease	Decrease
(E)	Decrease	No change

11. Which of the following is true of an import quota? It

(A) is a tax on imported goods.

(B) limits quantity of imports allowed into a country.

(C) will decrease the price of imported goods.

(D) will raise revenue for the government.

(E) helps to address a balance of trade surplus.

12. If real interest rates in the United States increase relative to real interest rates in other countries, which of the following will occur?

(A) Capital will flow out of the United States.

(B) The demand for loanable funds in the United States will increase.

(C) The supply of loanable funds will increase in other countries.

(D) The supply of loanable funds will increase in the United States.

(E) The demand for loanable funds will increase in other countries.

13. Which of the following will lead to an increase in the demand for loanable funds in the United States?

(A) A decrease in the real interest rate in the United States

(B) An increase in household savings

(C) An increase in U.S. government borrowing

(D) An increase in the supply of loanable funds in other countries

(E) A decrease in the supply of loanable funds in the United States

14. If the U.S. dollar appreciates in the foreign exchange market, U.S. imports and exports are most likely to change in which of the following ways

	U.S. imports	U.S. exports
(A)	Increase	Remain unchanged
(B)	Increase	Increase
(C)	Increase	Decrease
(D)	Decrease	Remain unchanged
(E)	Decrease	Decrease

15. In the United States, an increase in which of the following will cause an increase in U.S. imports?

I. Per capita real income

II. Price level

III. Real interest rates

IV. Tariffs

(A) I and II only

(B) I and III only

(C) I and IV only

(D) I, II, and III only

(E) II, III, and IV only

16. Which of the following will occur if inflation in the United States begins to rise while prices in other countries remain relatively stable? In the United States,

(A) the current account moves toward surplus.

(B) net exports rise.

(C) real interest rates decrease.

(D) the dollar appreciates.

(E) there is a capital outflow.

17. Suppose that the price level in Country A increases relative to the price level in other countries. In which of the following ways are Country A's imports and exports most likely to change?

	Country A's imports	Country A's exports
(A)	Increase	No change
(B)	Increase	Decrease
(C)	No change	Decrease
(D)	No change	Increase
(E)	Decrease	Increase

18. In the short run, in which of the following ways is an expansionary monetary policy most likely to cause the real interest rate and the value of the domestic currency to change?

	Real interest rate	Value of currency
(A)	Increase	Increase
(B)	Increase	Decrease
(C)	No change	Decrease
(D)	Decrease	Increase
(E)	Decrease	Decrease

19. If expansionary fiscal policies in the United States lead to increased budget deficits, what will happen to real interest rates in the United States and the value of the dollar?

	Real interest rate	Value of the dollar
(A)	Increase	Increase
(B)	Increase	Decrease
(C)	No change	Decrease
(D)	Decrease	Increase
(E)	Decrease	Decrease

20. If real interest rates in the United States are increasing faster than real interest rates in other countries, which of the following is most likely to occur?

(A) The demand for dollars will decrease, and the value of the dollar will increase.

(B) The demand for dollars will increase, and the value of the dollar will increase.

(C) The supply of dollars will decrease, and the value of the dollar will increase.

(D) The supply of dollars will increase, and the value of the dollar will increase.

(E) The supply of dollars will increase, and the value of the dollar will decrease.